A FRENCH OFFICER'S
DIARY

T0352316

France and North Africa

(This map shows the author's itinerary; maps of the scenes of battle will be found at the end of the book)

A FRENCH OFFICER'S DIARY

(23 AUGUST 1939—1 OCTOBER 1940)

BY

D. BARLONE

of the Free French Forces,
formerly Captain 2nd North African Division

Translated from the French

by

L. V. CASS, M.A.

With a Preface by

GENERAL P. L. LEGENTILHOMME

CAMBRIDGE

AT THE UNIVERSITY PRESS

1942

CAMBRIDGE UNIVERSITY PRESS
Cambridge, New York, Melbourne, Madrid, Cape Town,
Singapore, São Paulo, Delhi, Tokyo, Mexico City

Cambridge University Press
The Edinburgh Building, Cambridge CB2 8RU, UK

Published in the United States of America by
Cambridge University Press, New York

www.cambridge.org
Information on this title: www.cambridge.org/9781107600294

First published 1942
First paperback edition 2011

A catalogue record for this publication is available from the British Library

ISBN 978-1-107-60029-4 Paperback

PREFACE

A French Officer's Diary, the title which Major Barlone has chosen for the publication in English of his War Diary, is an extremely vivid story of a French Unit from the mobilization in 1939 to the collapse of France in 1940 and the subsequent demobilization after the Armistice.

However, the author does not stop at this tragic phase of our history, but continues his story up to the moment when he was able to join General de Gaulle's Free French Forces in England.

This diary, which, I think, is the first to be published by a Free French Officer, makes an extremely interesting contribution towards comprehension of the drama which was played out in France. The story will be fascinating for those who did not themselves live through it as well as for those who played a part.

The reader will live himself the life of those French soldiers who, sent to the frontier in 1939 and left inactive during eight months, could not believe that the horrors of war could ever again spread over our country. The awakening was brutal when, suddenly, Holland and Belgium were attacked. The advance of our armies across the fields of Flanders brought with it the hope of finishing once and for all with the Germans on a field of battle chosen by the French High Command and known to everyone. Doubt arose when it became apparent that no defences had been prepared over a battlefield stretching from Anvers to Namur, but our soldiers fought with heroism in a situation which was rapidly considered hopeless.

The simplicity of the author's style brings home to us the stupefaction of our troops confronted by an avalanche of disasters. Then, after a brief stay in England, he describes the return to France and the last dying efforts before the Armistice and the Demobilization. At once the question arose which troubled the conscience of every Frenchman, the question which is still being asked to-day in France: Is the game definitely lost? Which is the way of honour?

And it was thus that on 18 June 1940 and on the following days that General de Gaulle's solemn and resolute appeal was heard from London, an appeal which Major Barlone and many others have answered. His voice replied to the questions everyone was asking himself: Hope is reborn in French hearts—The fight continues—France is fighting still—France will be with the Allies at the final victory.

P. L. LEGENTILHOMME
Général de Division
Commissaire National à la Guerre.

London, 5 August 1942

AUTHOR'S NOTE

These notes from my war diary have helped me to keep a clear picture of events from the day I was called up until my arrival in England. They give some idea of my own reactions and those of people around me.

Many of my judgments have since proved erroneous; but I have not revised or moderated them, believing that the sole merit of these short notes lies in the fact that they record what I saw, felt and heard.

D. BARLONE

To

GENERAL DAME

who died of wounds while a prisoner of war
in Germany; and to my comrades, officers
and men of the 2nd North African Division,
who fell for the cause of freedom in the
Battle of France.

A FRENCH OFFICER'S
DIARY

23 *August* 1939.   France has been quite bewildered for the
last few days; Germany and Soviet Russia have just concluded
a pact of non-aggression whilst our Military Mission together
with the British is at Moscow, at Stalin's request, to seek agreement with the Red Staff as to possible operations in the event of
war. This *volte-face* is being very severely criticized by all the
Press except naturally the Communists, who nevertheless are
very much embarrassed and unable to give a satisfactory ex-
planation.

Daladier proclaims that exceptional military measures will
have to be taken in the near future; one senses a complete re-
versal of the situation in favour of Germany, without however
believing that the position is desperate. Munich in September
1938 and the startling news of March and May have blunted the
edge of public opinion. People refuse to envisage the situation
except through the tiny peep-hole of Danzig, and a war for 'this
provincial town' as Hitler called it, in an attempt to conceal his
intentions, would be unthinkable.

Meanwhile, the German press gives vent to more and more
exorbitant claims on the Provinces of Posen and Silesia and in-
vents 'persecution' of the Germans living in Poland.

My sister and I, on the contrary, have long since believed in
the inevitability of the struggle. So I was not surprised when at
four o'clock, she telephoned me at my office in Paris that two
soldiers had just brought my calling-up notice.

I say good-bye to Benjamin and to the employees, who fully
believe that I shall be back at the office by next week. Hastily I
make a few purchases: some stout boots, an electric torch, etc.
...I met de Chaunac, then Samson, a very intelligent German
Jew, both of whom arrange to meet me in a fortnight's time.

Mobilization

'So you don't believe that there is going to be a war?' I said to the latter. 'How could anyone believe in any such thing?' he replied; 'France is not ready; she has nothing to go to war with; she would be crushed in a couple of weeks; France will not commit that piece of folly, believe me.'

I shook hands with him without saying a word, amazed to hear such an opinion, for all the German Jews that I have known in recent times urge war like veritable madmen.

24 *August* 1939.   I take leave of my sister, who is very brave and, as usual, full of energy. Once more I advise her to leave Paris, since no other ties exist to keep her there. She prefers to remain, she isn't afraid. We feel sad, however, believing war to be inevitable. We do not doubt our victory, but wonder what price we shall have to pay.

The train for Toul is full of officers and men; the men as usual joke and laugh. The officers talk to each other about their particular branch of the service. I lunch in the dining-car next to a young lieutenant in the infantry on his way to the Maginot Line. He tells me that he has travelled considerably in Germany for his Insurance Company; only a few weeks ago he did a round there. We agree in thinking that the shortage of food, supposed to exist there, is all eye-wash. He also believes in a long and hard war, and in the swift crushing of Poland. His company is detailed to occupy a gap between two works of the Maginot Line.

We arrived at Toul about four o'clock in the afternoon. The barracks, named after Joan of Arc, stand at the other end of the town. There, I am told to take command of the 92/20 Horse Transport Company of the Headquarters of the 2nd North African Division whose Staff is stationed at Dommartin-les-Toul, a suburb quite near to the barracks. I take possession of the *Journal de Mobilisation* of my company, a bulky volume, which tells me what I have to do and what stores I have to draw day by day. Much work and all perfectly planned. I plunge into this mass of work, endeavouring to get my bearings.

At the local town hall, where I set up my office, I meet Lieutenant Bloch (from Sarreguemines). He is very short, freckled and quite bald, always smiling, and has a pronounced Lorraine

accent; always surrounded by friends who remember his cheerfulness on field-days. Good, I'll make him my assistant, I think
that we shall get on well together.

Then Second Lieutenant Viry, very correct, very young and
serious. He introduces himself to me at the regulation four
paces. He has just completed his training in the regular army
and was recalled a week ago, as a nucleus for the formation of the
company. He has the 'hippo' (horse transport) service at his
finger ends, and seems to have a certain contempt for me when I
tell him that I know nothing about it, having always served in
the infantry and in mechanized units. As he contemplates my
temples touched with grey, my old uniform now out of fashion,
I feel that he is thinking, 'We're doing fine with an old guy like
that'. We shall see....

I am lodging with mother Maquin—82 years old—a nice old
woman whose son is a ranker Major of Tirailleurs Algériens
(Algerian Rifle Regiment). Mother Maquin is terribly gossipy
and very lively, and she tells me all her troubles. Everybody
calls her 'Aunty', a nickname I suppose, but she tells me that
she has thirty-two nephews and nieces in this tiny village.

She must have reserved my bed for a flea-breeding ground,
for in the morning, after a sleepless night, I notice that hundreds
of swellings adorn my body. Well, I suppose it can't be helped!

The old dame is delighted, as I have lent Martin, my batman,
to her. He is a fine hard-working farmer of the district. I've
also lent her a few other poilus to shake her plum trees, loaded
with mirabelles. For four years there have been no mirabelle
plums and now that is the only thing that matters in the
countryside. Mother Maquin stuffs my pockets full of them, and
I eat enough to make me ill.

The men of the reserve come in without undue haste, without
the enthusiasm of 1914, or even that of last year, being fully
persuaded that they will be sent home in two weeks' time, and
annoyed at not being able to complete the harvest. But if one
has to go—of course, one will go, and return home to peace and
quietness after having given Hitler a good drubbing. The men's
great hope is that Hitler will be assassinated because, for the
time being, they separate Hitler in their minds from Germany.

Lack of war aims

Once he is beaten, so they reason, all will be over. They do not realize that Hitler is the manifestation of Germany's predatory instinct, the incarnation of the chosen people whose mission is to dominate the world. Nor do they realize that he is the Leader elected by plebiscite with eighty million votes behind him, of which nine-tenths are probably genuine; that he is also probably the leader of a conspiracy by three great bandits, three devouring monsters: Hitler himself, Mussolini and Japan, and that these are leagued together like gangsters in an attempt to plunder two rich and prosperous nations, the only two who can pay with their immense colonial empires: England and ourselves.

The calmness and the lack of pervasive enthusiasm of our soldiers is moreover due—and this is serious—to the fact that, apart from a desire not to be uprooted every six months, they have no war aims of territorial conquests; but they have one very definite aim, that of finishing off Hitler once and for all. In 1914—when enthusiasm was unbounded—there was in our hearts after, but only after, war had been declared, the will to reconquer Alsace and Lorraine and a desire for revenge. From the start, France was invaded; we had to retake the lost provinces and free our native soil.

But to-day we desire nothing; we have more than enough colonies, we know that our land is safe from invasion, thanks to the Maginot Line; no one has the least desire to fight for Czecho-Slovakia or for Poland, of which ninety-five Frenchmen out of every hundred are completely ignorant and unable to find on a map; we have no belief that Hitler will hurl himself on us after having swallowed up the little nations, one by one. We tell ourselves that having obtained what he wants, he will leave us in peace.

But the Germans have stupendous war aims; the recovery of what they lost through the treaty of Versailles; to own colonies; to wipe out defeat; to regain their pride; to dominate the world. They scorn the democracies; they have unlimited confidence in their military power and the successes of Hitler have swollen them with pride and self-assurance. Truly these are the war aims of jackals, but offensive aims, whilst ours are merely defensive.

Organizing the unit

Here the Germans have a considerable advantage over us from the point of view of morale.

25 *August* 1939.   We begin to collect harness, arms, stores and rations, etc. The requisitioning parties send us fine horses quite unused to sleeping tethered in the open.

An officers' mess is established in a little restaurant half-way between the Jeanne D'Arc barracks and Dommartin; the tables are laid for eighteen to twenty men. We are still cold and reserved in the mess.

Bets are made on the chances of the war. Here, as elsewhere, no one believes that it will come to anything, and the stakes are low and few. I refrain for fear of revealing my pessimism.

28 *August* 1939.   From six in the morning until dark I have been busy organizing my unit, forming teams of horses, etc. Things are shaping well. I believe that I shall have a good batch of N.C.O.s: most important. Stifling heat. Mother Maquin's fleas frightfully aggressive!

30 *August* 1939.   My company is now more or less complete. I have a new second lieutenant, Desouches, very Parisian, charming and handsome. He is tall, elegant, distinguished and sporting, like an English public schoolboy. He is a coal-man, he tells me, and by that he means that his father is one of the great proprietors of the Ivry coal-depôts. His wife has been to see him; he was able to lunch with her and he came back—in tears; tears that tell that it would have been better if his wife had not come. His grief, so youthful and genuine, attracts my sympathy. I feel we shall soon be friends.

Viry, I learn, is training for the priesthood. He has displayed intense activity. He is bursting to do his bit and is gradually losing his reserve with me, for he sees the trouble that I am taking. He even expresses gratitude to me. Later we shall become firm friends.

Bloch, a dealer in hides and leather at Sarreguemines, is unfailingly cool and unruffled (the Israelite and the priest-to-be will get on well together, I think). In the last war he was in the German army, but thanks to his proved pro-French attitude, he was allowed to take the officer's course, and became second lieutenant, then lieutenant. He is well-educated, pleasant to talk to and we see eye to eye; he believes there will be war and that it will be terribly hard, but is confident of our victory.

Next comes our veterinary officer, Captain Lefevre, from Villiers-sur-Mer. He is very gentle and an old campaigner too. Then the M.O., an Alsatian, Major Frey, a homœopath from Nancy, sprightly and bespectacled, perhaps a little muddle-headed, but a decent enough fellow. He had wandered about miserably for four days trying to find a billet. Through some mistake he had not been posted anywhere; the doctor who was supposed to come to me not having materialized, I adopted Frey—he gave me the impression of a dog looking for his master.

31 *August* 1939. In the afternoon I received the order to entrain with part of my company. The rest will follow tomorrow in two train-loads. I leave Toul at six o'clock in the evening with the hospital unit and some of the staff officers of the division.

Entraining is a difficult operation. Fifteen to twenty men have to hoist, clinging to the spokes of the wheels, to manhandle our heavy vehicles, then manœuvre them on to the trucks, utilizing all possible space; then there are the service wagons, the forage wagons and the light carts. In spite of the fact that our men have not worked together before, those of our officers who know how to do this work have formed teams who acquit themselves much better than I could have expected, but I wasn't too happy at first. Our men are already becoming attached to the material that they handle; it is theirs after all.... Our farm workers deal gently with the horses. Those that are restive are entrained by means of a sling: a rope is passed round the hind legs, just above the hocks. Two men at each end pull the horse in the direction of the truck. The animal cannot lash out, and it yields to the blandishments of the man at its head who gently leads it into the truck. All is going well; I am in charge of this huge train.

We arrive at Mangiennes, to the south of Thionville. It is midnight and the rain is beating down in inky darkness. Detrain-ing very awkward as there is no platform. Carts and wagons are unloaded by skidding off. No accidents. I spend the rest of the night with Captain Lefevre and a few of our men on some hay in a barn.

1 *September* 1939. At 7 a.m. departure for Pillon, a large village 3 miles away. The ambulance unit, commanded by the doctor, Major Rougetet, accompanies us; he is a good fellow, very homely. Excellent relations all round from the first. I get on with the billeting of my company, including the two sections due to join us at the station of Danvilliers on the following evening. They detrain by the light of powerful acetylene lamps which shed a fantastic light over all: orders, calls, shouting, pygmies straining at Herculean labours, scared horses, kicking and rearing, blinded by the fearful glare of the lights.

These twenty-four hours spent in a train in torrid heat and the hard work have worn out men and horses, at present out of training.

Life at Pillon is organized on the lines of the annual camp. Roll calls, inspection of arms, guard duties, plus one special observation post in the tower of the church, our old Saint-Etienne. Machine guns are mounted for anti-aircraft defence.

2 *September* 1939. At midday I find the good lady of the house, in which I have a pretty little room, in tears. The wireless has just announced the general mobilization and her husband was called up, like the rest of us, a few days ago. This extremely grave measure causes little emotion among civilians and soldiers, who are now getting used to the idea of a war, though still refusing to believe it to be inevitable. In the evening my hostess is calm and smiling. Our mess is installed in a forester's cottage. The forester has been called up, and his wife, half crazy, cries and laughs together. Dr Frey is made chief messing officer, to his great joy, for he likes his eats and likes them good.

Every day, as C.O. of a unit, I report to General Lescanne, the Divisional Commander, at 10 a.m. He is thin, turning grey, hair scanty, old-fashioned moustache, nearly white, rejoicing in a Lorraine accent. Viewed from the back, he looks like a second lieutenant. With a mind that is clear-cut, methodical and calm, he questions each in turn on our quarters and our needs, and listens to our suggestions. I note that some equipment seems to be lacking and will be required by the Infantry and the Artillery before they will be really ready. For a shock division such as ours (13th and 22nd Algerian Riflemen, 11th Zouaves, 40th and 240th Artillery, anti-tank batteries, pioneers, engineers, ambulances, etc.) the equipment in clothing, arms, munitions, tools, vehicles is incomplete: considerable progress however on what I saw last September. It was disastrous, scandalous. Daladier and his team have really made gigantic efforts in the past year. How should we come off if we had to start the fray now? We should manage somehow, I suppose, as always; General Lescanne doesn't seem to be very alarmed. In 1914–18 it was worse and we pulled through. Personally I should be happier if we had all the necessary gear. On returning to Pillon, I keep my fears from my officers. Why put doubt in their minds?

At once, at these meetings, the intelligent officers can be distinguished from the others, the broad-minded from the sticklers for authority. The staff officers, with the exception of two or three, seem to fall short of their job; the chief staff officer in particular, Colonel Dumoncel. Colonel Simon, in command of the Divisional Infantry (he limps badly—a legacy of 1914–18), hardly ever speaks, but his judgment and clear-headedness are sound. Colonel Bignon, the Artillery C.O., and Captain Perrier, Chief of 'Operations' (he stammers, but knows what he wants), inspire me with confidence. Some brains luckily, but Dumoncel is not one of them.

On the whole, this officers' meeting is pointless and has no interest for me; it is probably indispensable to the General in order to effect contact between the different units of the division.

The mess is rotten, a bad cook, there'll be a change soon. I don't want to attach too much importance to these details. The M.O. acknowledges that he is incapable of giving orders; he hasn't the manner or the ability.

4 *September* 1939. Sometimes at the officers' meetings rather

amusing details crop up. In a tiny town the use of the church bells had been limited to sound the alert. On Sunday, when they rang for evensong, the whole population, civil and military, rushed to the trench-shelters. The General has decided that henceforth a bugle only shall be used to sound the alert.

The Assistant Provost Marshal, a worthy gendarme, re-engaged second lieutenant, has decided off his own bat to suppress all car lighting at night time. Result: the following day—a hecatomb of cars and lorries. As there is no official guidance, the General decided to follow the advice of the previous day's *Paris-Soir*, namely to drive with side lights or with lights dipped. Fine! We now depend on *Paris-Soir* for our inspiration. The General laughs about it, but the Provost looks down his nose.

We spend four days at Pillon, happy as boys in camp, with our little schemes and the usual gossip.

5 *September* 1939. The whole division sets out on the road, after dark, for fear of planes. With our horses and drivers still unused to the convoys, each climb is sheer purgatory, each descent an acrobatic feat. We look like a tribe of gypsies and Desouches dubs me 'The king of the Romanis'. These convoys remind me of the last war—I've been on leave for twenty years....And here we are rolling along until midnight or 1 a.m. and even until ten or eleven the next morning, constantly being held up and with innumerable halts. Then I go ahead to see what is the matter; sometimes it is an infantry regiment, with all its accompanying gear, sometimes a convoy of artillery, a mile long, which has come to a standstill in front of us; wagons, guns, trucks, horses, men, doltish, passive, silent, asleep, standing by the ditch-side. A few of them enjoy a smoke and talk softly.

Are these dumb shadows emerging from the night for a few seconds the men I knew in the last war, the dead rising to stride to the front to wreak their vengeance on the Hun, to finish the work that we didn't end? Are they the new generation, marked by destiny as the victims of this war? Are they not rather fleeting shadows, wraiths whom night robs of being and substance?

Then a long way off a muffled noise is heard; it grows and grows in the night; the journey has begun once more. The vast river thaws, block by block the thaw comes nearer to us, whistles sound shrilly, wheels creak, drivers shout. On to the next stop? Why does one stop? No one will ever know.

About two o'clock in the morning we halt for a meal, the cooks pass along the column distributing the bread ration, a tin of bully-beef to every four or five men, and the coffee that they have prepared in the field kitchen en route. Everyone has a snack and will be able to hold out until daylight. My officers and I make for the field kitchen. The 'juice' is hot and good, a tin of meat or sardines is opened; we joke and smoke a cigarette. Oh! All's well. Nothing to report, the men's spirits are high.

To reach the region of Hayanges (Hagondanges) we cross the valley of Briey. At Banvilliers-Monts, where we spend the day, official and commercial notices are in three languages, French, German and Polish. Miners with helmets on and lamp in hand make their way along the streets. This is one of those areas which was never bombarded by the French artillery and planes in the last war and this despite the fact that from the earliest days it had fallen into the hands of the Germans, who were thus able to extract without hindrance incredible quantities of iron to melt down into guns and shells. When you stand there, and see so clearly the military objectives within reach, you are reduced to wondering what could possibly be the key to the mystery. Ancient stories of mutual agreements between manufacturers of armaments on the one hand and German and allied military staffs, whose headquarters were never bombed, come to mind.

I impart some of my thoughts to Desouches, but I see that I worry him, and I have no business to do this. To put matters right, I turn everything into a joke; after all, he is young and care-free, and seemingly thinks no more about it. But if the war lasts long, if we suffer reverses, if these stories or others are brought out once more, he will remember my words. I feel remorseful, and all the more so, because even if such things are true, I shall continue to do my duty just as in the last war.

Each night we push over towards the right; at Mangiennes we faced Luxemburg, now we are south of the Sarre. After a particularly hard day's march to reach the tiny village of Rurange, we arrive in torrential rain at 2 a.m. We spend the next day there until nightfall, then on to the Maginot Line through the marshes of Gommelange-Bettange. We skirt some huge earth-works which seem to me very strong. But I am amazed to see that nothing, absolutely nothing, has been prepared in depth, neither in the rear, nor in the 6 to 8 miles separating them from the frontier. The Maginot Line is a single thread, 100 or 150 yards wide, including a ridiculous network of barbed wire, to-gether with upturned ends of some rails stuck in the earth in the foreground to stop, so it appears, tanks. But supposing one or two of the works unfortunately fall? How will the men behind the Line be able to stem the flood which will pour through the gap and so outflank the forts? However, we have been told that an elastic system of defence, 30 miles deep, does exist, similar to that now being constructed in the Siegfried Line. Not in this sector at any rate! Desouches is riding at my side and I reveal my astonishment to him. He waxes quite indignant over my scepticism in regard to the solidity of the Line and tries to prove to me that if the works are protected by cross-fire from long-range guns, my fears would be vain, indeed quite improbable. I pretend to be convinced, perhaps he is right. Still, it is better to have two strings to one's bow, and the miles of defence in depth that we constructed in 1914 came to my mind. After all, our war lords must also be mindful of this, and they are certainly better qualified than I.

11 *September* 1939. Holling. Arrived at Holling in driving rain, the night was as black as ink. Like all villages situated in front of the Maginot Line it has been evacuated by order; the inhabitants had had half an hour in which to prepare seventy pounds of luggage to take with them in the military lorries waiting for them. That was to be the sum total of their worldly goods.

In the course of the day I go for a walk in this charming Lorraine village, situated in the valley of the Nied which flows quite near by. The houses are large and opulent, the wide streets are bordered by the inevitable dung-heaps, dear to Lorraine. Countless herds of cows and pigs wander through the streets and fields. Our orders are to live on the produce of the country.

Living on the country

Those of my men who are farm workers, and they are numerous, know what to do, only too pleased to resume something of their peace-time job. There are 800 to 900 men to be billeted in the homes of 250 inhabitants, as the Ambulance Section and the Artillery are quartered with us. Gangster methods are used to obtain the finest animals; soon my stable housed 30 superb pigs and 20 dairy cows, looked after by volunteer cowherds. That is our reserve; for immediate use we kill stray animals in the woods and in the fields. Everywhere friendly groups of men rig up their cook-houses; throughout the day the squeals of doomed pigs and poultry can be heard, whilst other men go off to thrash the walnut trees, shake down the mirabelles and the quetsches, unearth the 'spuds', uproot the salads. My men feed sumptuously, pastry-cooks make flans with the flour, found in abundance, and butter made in the dairy. This is the land of milk and honey.

The 'clearing up' goes on apace. I am taken, very secretly, to visit a still set up by the men. There they distil the contents of barrels of mirabelles and quetsches which the unlucky proprietors had put by. Within a few days we have in carboys more than a dozen gallons of wonderfully fragrant brandy. I intend keeping it for the days when things warm up.

Now the whirring of a threshing machine comes from a barn, and soon fifty sacks of good oats for our horses are lined up on our carts. No need to ask for volunteers, the N.C.O.s and skilled farm workers organize their teams and everything proceeds smoothly, no drunkenness, no quarrelling.

My headquarters are in the spacious café of the village. On the ground floor, in the large main room, the clerks play at Russian billiards when their work is done. The mess is behind. On the first floor is my bedroom, with marble wash-basin, handsome wardrobe, etc. Desouches has a horror of solitude, so he shares my room together with a magnificent Mechlin dog which is almost entirely white and has almond-shaped eyes, ringed with black. Desouches adopted this lovely creature from among hundreds straying about the village in search of their masters. Gradually they all find new masters. Desouches does not like getting up early, so when I go downstairs at six o'clock to go out, 'Tell', who has put his great head against my cheek, begs me to take him, which I do, much to his internal relief. When Desouches does indeed wake up, as he is susceptible to the cold, he remains beneath his eider-down and plays me a few tunes on his harmonica.

Holling church has been fitted up to receive the wounded. The chairs and pews on the left of the choir have been replaced by a boarded floor, bearing large notices at intervals: 'Seriously Wounded', 'Gassed', 'Extremely Urgent', 'Urgent'. On Sundays, officers and men squash together on the right side of the choir, the numerous officers in front. Beneath the priest's chasuble, I recognize the gaiters and heavy boots of an army medical corps sergeant who is officiating. The acolytes, two poilus. At the organ is a M.O. who has collected an excellent body of singers. During the whole service there is, in the background, the rumbling of nearby gunfire; the windows shake during communion. Nearly all the men have their prayer books; they haven't forgotten them, it is part of the few poor, but precious possessions packed away in their kits or haversacks. The religious fervour of all these worthy fellows, singing wholeheartedly, stirs my innermost feelings. I contemplate their young faces, tanned, clean-shaven this day, aglow with faith, their eyes shining as they think of God and of France too.

On coming out, the officers chat and laugh, pass on the news, invite each other to their mess. Then each one returns to his billet, some by car, others on horseback. In the evening we listen to the wireless in our café, giving news of the war in Poland and we refuse to believe in the smashing advance announced by the Germans. Besides, things will change.

14 *September* 1939. Every day I make my visit to General Lescanne's council meetings at his headquarters at Vaudechain, $2\frac{1}{2}$ miles in front of us, almost on the German frontier. There, I learn that our regiments take villages which the Germans hardly make an effort to defend. But the villages are riddled with booby-traps. Someone opens a cupboard door, or a chair is moved, and the house is blown up. So much so, that our 75's had to be used to destroy one village before we could enter it. We are preparing an attack which is destined to draw off the enemy and

thus relieve the pressure on the Poles. It will soon be launched. Every night I hear unending streams of artillery, munitions, aircraft supplies passing beneath my window. Each night we receive orders to take barbed wire and pickets, pit props, etc., to the engineers for the work that they are carrying out in fortifying the conquered territory. One night our detachment was shelled, though not heavily, by German artillery. Viry, who was in command, asked for twenty volunteers to complete the work. Fifty offered themselves. That was sporting of men who had just received their baptism of fire. Now while riding each day over the lovely wooded hills which overlook the Nied, I run up against camouflaged guns, munition dumps, the emplacement of an observation balloon in course of construction, etc. Every place is crammed full of guns of all sizes, air-force, pioneers, sappers and so on. The C.C.S. is ready to receive batches of 600 wounded. The attack is on the point of being launched—that is as clear as day. The Polish front will be eased. We are all burning with desire and jumping for joy at the idea of entering the fray. And we shall see if the Siegfried Line will stand up to our pounding, for the pounding of the French Artillery, such as I saw in 1917 and 1918, was something to be reckoned with. This time it will be much more severe.

Holling is on an exposed road leading to the front. The Germans will counter-attack and the road will inevitably come under their fire. I am going to reconnoitre some positions where we shall be able to put the men, horses and reserve vehicles under cover, at four to five hundred yard intervals, when the shelling begins. I must also be prepared for a check to our attack and a successful German counter-attack; for to be more than half a mile ahead of the Maginot Line is like being caught in a mouse trap—it is impossible to cross over the Line through the fields because of the barbed wire and the anti-tank traps. One is forced to keep to the roads which alone are clear. But the roads are narrow, they will be terribly shelled, littered up with wounded men, and with troops going up or returning. So I look out for ditches, hollows and folds of the ground near the Maginot Line where I can camouflage my company while awaiting a free passage along a road.

The end of Poland

18 *September* 1939.   The Divisional Headquarters whisper to me that the attack begins to-morrow or the day following. I increase the number of exercises in harnessing at the double. At first, we took an hour, now everything is harnessed and loaded up in less than twenty minutes, and the wagons are more than 300 yards from the road. Not so bad.

Daladier spoke on the wireless two days ago. You should have seen my clerks' passionate interest while listening to him. The *Marseillaise* was played at the end, and many eyes glistened with tears while the brave lads stood rigidly to attention. I think that at this moment, millions of men and women, in France, in the Maginot Line, in billets, and in barracks, in Paris, in the most distant villages, are consumed by the same flame of love for France and the certainty of victory.

The news from Warsaw is disastrous; will our intervention be in time? When the Stuttgart traitor broadcasts his tall yarns and heavy jokes, what bursts of sarcastic laughter come from our men; this so-called Frenchman has not our style, he is completely Germanized—'bochified'.

19 *September* 1939.   The Russians have just attacked Poland. Why? To share the spoils, or to stop the German hordes? Poland is done for; since yesterday activity has slowed down, no more artillery, no fresh troops. The Staff give me to understand that the offensive will not take place. What a pity that nearly a fortnight has been wasted before being able to attack.

24 *September* 1939.   The troops retire gradually to the other side of the Line. The munition dumps are broken up.

We have little to do so Viry has introduced Sunday amusements for our men: concerts in a barn, football, horse-racing (using our clumsy farm animals), hunting the rose. In this last game a cluster of ribbons is tied to a rider's shoulder; the rider twists and turns about times without number in order to escape, the man who seizes his flower must fix it to his own shoulder and in turn be chased.   Reward to the winners; a bottle of wine, naturally.

Enemy shelling

30 *September* 1939.   All the troops have been withdrawn to positions behind the Maginot Line. Only reconnaissance squads, the eyes of the division, hold the front, withdrawing little by little until relieved by another division. These men are our antennae, and our shield, they prepare our advance or cover our retreat, acting as a very mobile but thin screen, being able to put up an intense fire from their automatic weapons. We are evacuating the ground taken from the Boche. Is this good tactics, I wonder? The Boche is showing himself more aggressive now. Captain Vinchon, of the reconnaissance squad, held a German village; it received 500 shells—105's—in half an hour, he had to retire, and the enemy then occupied it. But during the night Vinchon retook the village by means of hand-grenades. Thirteen killed altogether. Vinchon is a notary of Rheims, one of the best. We lunched together a week ago.

1 *October* 1939.   The General and his Headquarters' Staff withdrew several days ago. We are the last element of the division to remain behind, protected by the divisional reconnaissance screen. I receive the order to retire a few miles and billet at Bettange, upon the edge of the great Gommelange marsh which forms a part of the Maginot Line. The whole plain can be inundated in a few hours if attacked. We take away the remainder of our pigs in our wagons; a few soldiers drive our cows and calves along the roads.

5 *October* 1939.   The 32nd Infantry Division has ended its occupation of the sector that we have just quitted. They were enlisted in Lunel near Montpellier. Some of the men are regular 'Tartarins', ready to accomplish the most amazing exploits; however, since our voluntary retirement from the frontier, complete calm reigns throughout the sector.

Tactically I think that we have done well in not hanging on to the few miles that we had taken in Germany. Had we been able to help Poland, they would have served as a taking-off point, but in themselves they were of no consequence. The Germans would have done their utmost in order to be able to say that not an inch of the Fatherland was being trampled by the enemy. There would have been much slaughter without any practical result.

The division is now in reserve, my company is billeted at the large farm of Leoville, near Courcelles-Chaussy, with the Army Service Corps, which from there serves the whole division. I have never seen mud like this since 1914; one sinks in it up to the ankles. Except for the horses, that I manage to shelter in sheds, these are poor quarters. A badly chosen spot; three to four hundred vehicles pass along the unmetalled roads from six in the morning until three in the afternoon, in full sight of the German planes, which have already paid us some photographing visits. So, when General Lescanne came to see us one afternoon and asked me what I thought of the quarters, I replied, 'As bad as can be, General'. 'That is my opinion too', he replied. 'Look out for another billet with more cover at once.' On the morrow I proposed Les Etangs, a charming shady village, very near to the refilling station. I went and had a word with the billeting officer, and we moved in on 12 October, the troops already there closing up.

Every night our transport goes backwards and forwards between the station and the village, a distance of a mile, to unload at the barns the rations for the division. Each unit will send for its supplies the next morning. Quite a nice little job for us, finishing between midnight and one in the morning.

I have paid a visit to the Chateau d'Urville at Courcelles-Chaussy, a gift from the town of Metz to the Kaiser, who used to spend a few days there each year. A fine park, but the chateau is in bad German taste. Like the one at Londonvillers, quite near, it is impossible to imagine a more mixed accumulation of styles of all ages. A hospital is installed there. There too, the park is rather beautiful, and is a part of the State forest. On the days when a deluge of rain is not descending, I like to ride in the hilly forest land around Londonvillers. One day I was with Lieutenant Ferry, a charming companion of the Motor Transport Company, a solicitor from Toul and fond of riding. We were following a little stream between steep banks when the ground became so soft that I advised him to follow me up the slope. Hardly had we gone thirty yards when Ferry, who was a little distance away, shouts out 'You're right, my horse is bogged'. I halted and turning saw Ferry's mount lying on its side, its legs completely buried. At the same moment I notice that my feet are touching the ground, my horse having gently sunk into the ground up to its belly. Shall I also sink into the mud on dismounting? No, the ground supports me. We let our horses regain breath for a few minutes, then having placed some brushwood under our feet, we help our poor beasts to get out of the mire by tugging at their heads. But we were rather scared, for night was falling and we were 4 or 5 miles from any habitation in that great forest.

20 *October* 1939.   Nothing to report since our arrival at Les Etangs. Life goes on monotonously, but according to plan.

The war starts up again with a few isolated air combats and an occasional surprise attack of no importance. It seems that time is on the side of the Allies. Let us hope so. Hitler, standing still, offers us plenty of scope for conjectures. It is generally said that he has been upset by the Allies' decision to stand by Poland. He thought that we should climb down once more; the German and Italian nations are against the war and are refusing to support Hitler and Mussolini; neither the Italian king nor the Italian nation wish to fight against France.

I do not believe a word of all this talk, for I have always been persuaded of the existence of a plan minutely worked out, between Italy, Germany, Japan and perhaps also Russia, who has now lined up against Poland. But when I try to put forward my point of view in the mess, I am met with a storm of protests and sarcastic remarks so, to break off, I pretend to be jesting. Result: we uncork two good bottles. Only Bloch takes no part in the discussions. I think that he shares my opinion.

1 *November* 1939.   All Saints' Day. The church overflowed with soldiers. I organized the trooping of the colours in the village. Later, we shall go up to the churchyard to pay homage to the men who fell in the last war, and to those, fortunately few in number so far, who have fallen in this. One of our N.C.O.s, Sergeant Hadamar, is buried there. The brave fellow had violent

internal pains, he wouldn't report sick for fear of being accused of malingering and he continued to toil along the roads. His operation for appendicitis was too late.

Before presenting arms at the graveside, all strewn with flowers, I spoke to the men something like this:

'We are all far from our own family graves. It is by remembering those of our elder brothers and of our comrades that we shall best fulfil our duty; for we owe it to them that the fate of Czecho-Slovakia and Poland is not ours. The torch has fallen from their dying hands into ours; ours is the duty to continue the struggle in order that France may continue to live always more beautiful, always greater. Let us remember, let us keep one minute of silence and let us think of our dead who have shown us the way in giving their lives for the Motherland.'

On turning around to let the men stand at ease, I see more than a dozen faces bathed in tears. The men's morale continues high, they are conscious of their duty and feel proud to belong to our magnificent 2nd North African Division. I never lose an opportunity of making them feel that this is an honour, and they understand me.

3 *November* 1939.   The General's Headquarters and the Divisional Headquarters are huddled together in the dreadful little village of Condé-Northen whose roads have nearly all been cut off by the floods. The General's council was held at first in the station waiting-room, then after a few days in the tiny schoolroom. This meeting becomes more and more futile; the General doles out, as in a sale room, the lists of clothing received by the Quartermaster and of the forms and tables made by the sappers for the men's quarters (I should have thought that the engineers would have been better occupied digging trenches and making entanglements. But that is not my business). We never learn anything about operations; only the most childish and unlikely hints to the effect that the Boches have got the wind up, that they are exhausted, and that Hitler is going crazy. I listen in astonishment, and turn away shrugging my shoulders.

10 *November* 1939.   The division falls back for a rest. Ac-

tually we are not tired, but by reason of a rota among all the divisions which occupy the front line one after another we are now sent to a reserve position behind the Maginot Line.

After fifteen hours of marching by night, we billet at Lesmesnil, near Pont-à-Mousson. On dismounting, I find my legs are somewhat stiff, but an hour later am all right again. There are only eleven houses or farms at my disposal for my company, the rest of the village being occupied by the 11th Zouaves. It is a puzzle to fix up all my people, and especially the 300 horses. The country-side was stripped in 1914–18. The barns, now rebuilt in concrete, are fortunately enormous, and airy. The horses are below, the men up above. In the course of one of my nightly rounds, which I make from time to time, I sit down in one of these barns which forms an excellent stable for sixty horses. For a long time I listen to these kindly animals munching their hay, their jaws making a continuous sound that lulls me nearly to sleep, and a gentle warmth spreads over my body. A calm feeling comes over me, my mind is at rest and in harmony with these beasts and men whose peaceful breathing I can hear. Then I wend my way beneath the star-strewn sky to my bed and sleep tranquilly, knowing that all my men are sleeping peacefully, trusting in the serenity and deep silence of the land.

17 *November* 1939.　We are so pinched for room, that I obtain permission from General Lescanne to look for billets at Loisy, about the same distance from Pont-à-Mousson. It is a clean and delightful little village at the foot of Sainte Geneviève's Hill, facing Le Prêtre wood. Men and horses are comfortable. Each day I ride out to a spur of Sainte Geneviève's Hill where one can still see the trenches of 1914, for fighting went on for four years at this spot. From the Chateau de Mousson, in ruins, there is a fine view. It is one of our favourite walks. Recently a chapel has been built there. In front of it there is a beautiful statue of Joan of Arc. The outstretched arms of the Maid seem to be protecting France from the invader. For the very first time I see, in the crevices of the old walls, colonies of thousands of ladybirds, like patches of red and black. During our visit to the ruins, we appoint 'Tell', Desouches' lovely dog, to guard the horses. It is

the first time that he has done this job, but immediately understood. His eyes follow us enviously, he would so like to frisk around us, but duty calls. From time to time, we call him to report to us; he leaps towards us. Then we tell him to return to guard his horses; he drops his tail, but goes back, and strangers going too close are not welcomed I assure you. What an intelligent dog!

No one talks of the war now. Winter is on its way and we are convinced that Hitler will not attack before the spring. From time to time the newspapers display great headlines announcing that an aeroplane has been brought down. The whole world seems to be unruffled. Shall we really have war? Or shall we remain facing each other, for years?

General Lescanne has held a great at-home, tea, bridge, the band of the 11th Zouaves. It was held in the fine chateau, where he is quartered with his staff. I meet crowds of friends. Buffet: first-class and abundant.

20 *November* 1939. Leave is now being given. There seems to be in existence behind the lines a Boche organization for spreading defeatist propaganda amongst our soldiers, so that the High Command has hesitated up to now to allow men to go to their homes. We receive orders to talk to the men and put them on their guard.

Would it not be simpler to put an end to German fifth column propaganda? I should be very astonished if fifth columnists were tolerated in Germany. But in France we are persuaded that Hitler trembles and will never attack us, and our government does not react with that violence which is characteristic of the Germans.

I would have thought that Daladier had more energy. If he is in bondage to his ideas of extreme liberty let him clear out.... To make war with peace-time methods and ideology is sheer nonsense!

What a pity if our fine boys at the front are corrupted by a canker—they, who would answer every call. If a clean-up is wanted, let them call upon us, and it will be done quickly.

We spend a month at Loisy. Then on 18th December comes

the order to entrain, by night. Fine ice-cold rain is falling. Apparently we are to go in the direction of Cambrai or Valenciennes. I fear that we shall never be so comfortable elsewhere as in this delightfully clean and hospitable village.

19 *December* 1939. We arrive at Maing, 4 miles to the south of Valenciennes; it is an agricultural village of 3000 inhabitants, some of whom are workers in the large factories at Valenciennes. The former Parish Council was dismissed, the mayor and his secretaries are under arrest for misappropriation of funds. The chief of the parish committee, nominated by the Prefect, is very patriotic and intelligent. He and the Curé point out to me a few propagandists who, however, are acting with extreme caution. I report to the Intelligence and to the military police, but they give me the impression that they do not take the matter seriously. The investigation is closed. I am annoying them.

Our men have a wonderful reception: the villagers, who have not had soldiers before, come and invite them in. All, or nearly all, sleep in beds.

22 *December* 1939. I go on leave to Toulon, to my niece Ghislaine. Paris, where I spend a day, looks just the same; there are few men and officers in the streets and in the underground.

The three relief trains for the Riviera are overcrowded. It is a good thing that I reserved my sleeping berth. My companion, a lieutenant in the Garde Mobile, and forty guardsmen have been serving with a reserve machine-gun company in order to smarten them up. He tells me that when war was declared, they had to hold a ridiculously long line without any serious support; for on the Luxemburg frontier we had built hardly any fortifications, the Maginot Line stopping at the German frontier. We trusted treaties of neutrality, and were completely unmindful of the fact that Germany is the country of scraps of paper. For some days, this lieutenant and his men remained practically cut off, then some cavalry regiments came to strengthen the front. But if the Germans had repeated their coup of 1914, they would have found nothing in front of them and would have penetrated as though through butter. Since those days, some hard work has been put in, in fortifying this sector.

Lovely weather at Toulon. I can often work all the morning in my pyjamas by the open window, looking out over the beautiful roadstead of Mourillon. The red globe of the rising sun leaves a gleaming white pathway over the sea on which hundreds of sea-gulls disport themselves. To the right the old fort of St Louis with Vauban's ramparts juts out into the sea, giving shelter to the delightful little port, where the boats are laid up. Fishermen drag their seines in front of my window.

When the batteries of Mont Faron fire in earnest, I can hear the huge shells whistling over the roof of the house, which vibrates. And now the guns of St Mandrier, hidden in the beautiful wooded hills facing us, join in the party. The barrage balloons mount in the sky. Seaplanes rise in flight, lifting immense columns of water, circle round, and then come to rest. The domes of enormous powder and munition depôts gleam in the sunshine. While this is going on, one has much more the impression of war than in the Maginot Line. Toulon teems with sailors and naval officers, whose great hope is one day to fight at the side of the English, whom they hold in great esteem and friendship, in contrast to the Italians, whom they despise profoundly.

The only infantry to be seen are the Senegalese. They are trained carefully in order to get them used to wear the heavy soldiers' boots. My nephew, Paul Guézé, adjutant to the Colonel of a new regiment at present in formation, tells me that they will soon cut as fine a figure as the old professional soldiers. These excellent fighters, who have shown fine courage and physical resistance in our colonies, can be used in Europe only during the fine season, because they succumb rapidly to the cold weather. During the winter they return to garrisons in the south of France.

Sunday. Exquisite lunch at Justin's at Carqueirane. A group of showy people from the Paris Stock Exchange lunch just behind us in the company of elegant women; rich motor-cars await them at the door. These people fill me with disgust.

In the evenings we often dine in the little eating-house of Toulon, where mussels farcies, exquisite bouillabaisse and other good things are served. Thanks to cocktails, good dinners and so on, one's money goes quickly. But life in the company of my sister, my niece and her two lovely children, her gaiety and her high spirits, is so pleasant. It is an effort to picture the severe, ugly, dark and cold life that I have left, and that I shall resume once more in three or four days, with my brave men, my mare and my friends.

26 *December* 1939. Naval officers tell us that they feel obliged to keep an eye upon their crews when their boats are in for repairs. The average mentality of the workers as well as of the country in general is excellent; they are patriotic, loyal and perhaps the best workmen in the world; but according to my informants a handful of misled people is always trying quite unconsciously to spread defeatist propaganda. The same thing has happened, so I was told, in Paris, at Hispano, Peugeot, Renault and other factories. Everywhere the overwhelming majority of the workers do their duty, working to the utmost of their capacity, but a few of them are led astray by hostile propaganda.

Everywhere people criticize the weakness of Daladier. It would be so easy to rid the workers, who ask nothing better, of the presence of these undesirables. The splendid morale of our sailors and soldiers must be preserved whatever the cost. If not, where should we be?

2 *January* 1940. On returning to Paris, I go and see André Reuze, the literary Editor of *Excelsior*, and Pierre Loiselet, Editor of *Vendémiaire*. Reuze and Loiselot confirm what I was told in Toulon. The propaganda of the Boche is centred chiefly on the metallurgists, with the help of a few foreigners, who seek, without much success, to break the morale and to destroy the patriotism of our French workers.

I am shocked and go to the War Office. I am politely received by a lieutenant who seemingly is interested in what I say to him. I suggest that three or four thousand agitators be rounded up and distributed in ones and twos among the units at the front on which one can rely. Instead of 80 or 100 francs a day, they would get 15 sous; the example would be salutary. He appears to take notes, thanks me and shows me out with a warm handshake. But I have the impression that as soon as the door is closed, he will throw in the waste-paper basket the few scrawls that he has so courteously made, for most probably he knows as much about the situation as I do, and perhaps the danger has been exaggerated. On the whole, the nation is absolutely all right; these few superficial signs of decay may not have, after all, the importance which we are inclined to attach to them.

10 *January* 1940. Intense cold and falls of snow. Luckily the house in which I live, in company with Desouches, and which also contains the mess, is very large, comfortable and well heated.

12 *January* 1940. All leave suspended: so I learn at Artres, the large château-farm, now our headquarters, where the officers' meetings are held under our new Commander, General Dame. The latter is young, alert, clean-shaven, with his hair brushed back. He is said to be a Freemason, and a social climber, but his bustling manner inspires one with confidence, and his intelligence and military knowledge are very sound, so we are assured. C.O.s have been recalled, for the entry of the Germans into Belgium is considered imminent; it is reported that an agreement with us was signed last night at Brussels, authorizing the Allies to cross the frontier as soon as the German attack begins.

In the evening, at 10 o'clock, I receive the order to stand by, ready to move off in two hours. All the men, roused from their sleep on an intensely cold night, are full of enthusiasm for the idea of going to fight the Germans at long last. When everything is loaded and the horses harnessed, the men turn in fully dressed.

16 *January* 1940.   General Dame indicates to us the general plan of campaign: The French army will defend the line Antwerp—Brussels—Namur. A light armoured division has already preceded us, but at G.H.Q. doubts exist about the efficiency of our armoured divisions compared with those of the Boches, which are more numerous. We seem to rely more on our infantry and artillery. Why? I have never been able to fathom the mystery.

18 *January* 1940.   The 'stand by' is now at an end. Each unit returns to its billet. Our men are very disappointed at not being able to get a knock at Jerry. Was there any real danger? It is believed that it was a manœuvre on the part of the British to wake up the Belgians, who are doing nothing to their fortifications, or to the positions that we shall have to occupy in front of Brussels if Germany attacks.

27–28 *January* 1940.   The thermometer drops to 36 degrees of frost. The roads are icebound and our horses are not able to move. Here we stick until the thaw.

31 *January* 1940.   Going out at 2 a.m., after playing bridge, Lieutenant Robert of the Air Force, blinded by the headlights of a car, falls into a ditch of ice-cold water. We wrap him up in rugs; after ten minutes' ride he will be at G.H.Q. at Artres, where he will find a warm bed.

5 *February* 1940.   All our available vehicles are placed at the service of the Engineers, who are building a series of blockhouses along the Belgian frontier. They are sited along an anti-tank ditch which, in its turn, is protected by a net-work of barbed wire and mine-fields right up to the very edge of this anti-tank ditch. Some of these fortifications have been constructed by civilian contractors who employ Italians, Belgians, Czechs. Furthermore, country-folk, inquisitive folk, and spies wander about continuously. No one makes any attempt to preserve any secrecy about our defences. The anti-tank ditches, whose

earth sides are retained merely by light wattles, appear very unpretentious. A quarter of an hour's bombardment and the earth would crumble away and would leave free passage, I fear, to any armoured vehicle, but they are a sufficient guaranty against a surprise attack.

I make frequent visits to view the workings, the progress of which is slow. The most surprising thing is that when the main works are completed they are neither armed nor guarded. Any one is free to enter, to sabotage anything and everything. When I diffidently make a remark to this effect to Captain Perrier of the General Staff, and Colonel Careme, a friend of his in the Engineers, they answer me confidentially, 'What are we to arm them with?'

First of all we must give the tools to our fighting units. In spite of the enormous increase in production, due to the intense patriotic efforts of the workers, neither guns nor anti-tank weapons are as yet issued in sufficient quantities. We do not receive enough of them to satisfy all our needs. The same remark applies to aviation. Certainly it takes a long time to organize the entire production of a big country. The High Command is to be blamed for this. It ought to have extended the Maginot Line to the sea, two years ago.

10 *February* 1940. Cold again, 18 degrees of frost! My company work with the Engineers, pouring concrete for the blockhouses. The Algerian riflemen give me the impression of not being able to stand up to so rigorous a winter, and consequently their training is slowed down. One is compelled to leave these officers and men inactive. The Boches, who have not our reasons for doing so, are undoubtedly not letting the grass grow under their feet.

Parliament is meeting in secret session; there is an indefinable sense of uneasiness. Public opinion would like France to intervene in the war in Finland. I doubt if we have the means. It is a long and difficult matter to organize an overseas expedition; it took us two years to get going at Salonika.

Roosevelt is sending his observer, Sumner Welles, to Europe. With what object?

A review at Valenciennes

11 *February* 1940.   The Russians increase their pressure on the Mannerheim Line, which is apparently broken.

12 *February* 1940.   Daladier obtained a vote of confidence at the secret session. So much the better. Perhaps we are inclined to exaggerate the situation behind the lines.

Twenty-seven degrees of frost during the night.

17 *February* 1940.   A Finnish request to Sweden for help has been refused. The Mannerheim Line seems to be cut. Cannot we do anything to help the Finns? It is an agonizing situation.

Yesterday there was a review in the square at Valenciennes and presentation of decorations by the Commander of the First Army—General Blanchard—a well set up man with a marked taste for photographers for whom he frequently poses. General de la Laurencie, commanding the Third Army Corps, and Colonel Sevestre of the 13th Algerian Rifles are created Commanders of the Legion of Honour. General Dame, our general, decorates many of the Algerian riflemen. We admire his youthful appearance. The square at Valenciennes, with its fine town hall nicely decorated, is well chosen for such a ceremony. The bands of the 11th Zouaves, 22nd and 13th Algerian Rifles march past, the latter being particularly good. Large crowds of cheering civilians.

18 *February* 1940.   Theatrical show for the troops in a large hall at Anzin. Our three Generals and some English guests preside at three successive shows. Singers, conjurors, clowns, Alibert, etc., and best of all Laura Diana who, in a few days' time, is marrying a flying officer; similarly Guy la Chambre married an old music-hall actress a few months ago.

We are doing all we can to keep up the spirits of the troops, in spite of the inaction. Cinema, once a week in billets, football teams everywhere, etc. Fine, but the best thing would be to carry on with training and work the men hard instead of letting them rust. These are, however, the orders from G.H.Q., so they must be obeyed.

Sumner Welles in Europe

20 February 1940.   I have been talking to some of the farmers at Maing, all good fellows and quite patriotic, but you realize the effect on them of successive devaluations of our currency. As soon as these countrymen have sold an animal they buy another and don't hesitate to say: 'We know that the franc is not worth much in spite of its fixed value, so we prefer to have cattle in our stables rather than keep banknotes.' I'm afraid it would be useless appealing to the French people, as in 1914, to hand over their gold and foreign securities to the Bank of France in exchange for savings certificates.

23 February 1940.   Daladier has made a statement to the Military Commission of the House. Wouldn't it be better to let them carry on rather than to try to satisfy their curiosity, some of them being rather doubtful characters? But Daladier knows them and I hope he only tells them as much or as little as he pleases.

27 February 1940.   Viborg has been taken by the Russians. We are told it is of no importance...indeed! Shall we do anything for Finland?

Sumner Welles, Roosevelt's representative, has commenced his trip round Europe. Apparently he is drawing up a plan for the resumption of economic relations after the war.

Very nice indeed, but we want planes and guns and not plans for the New York bankers and Chicago meat packers to carry on business, with nations drained of their blood and of their last bar of gold. At the very least it is useless: the Americans haven't the foggiest idea of the European situation!

29 February 1940.   The Finns seem to be at the end of their tether. It is too late now; neither we nor the English can do anything for that little handful of heroes. Too bad.

The French Government is going to publish another series of economic decrees. Shall we ever find our way through this avalanche of laws? We ourselves, in the Army, are deluged with paper work. I receive 30 to 40 papers a day notifying me of changes of one or two centimes in the scale of charges for coal, firewood, soap, candles, rations in kind or allowance. These changes are retrospective and make a Chinese puzzle. It seems unbelievable, but for seven months the rates of pay have never been stable; sometimes the pay is on one scale, sometimes on another. It seems that behind the lines everyone is expending his energy upon absurd and insignificant details. My poor pay-clerks are unknown heroes, for they somehow manage to wade through this mass of grotesque contradiction.

Sumner Welles is meeting Hitler to-day. Will that sinister comedian be brutal or coaxing? Rather the latter, to persuade Sumner Welles of the purity of his intentions.

1 *March* 1940. A brother officer from the 22nd Algerian Rifles lunches at the mess and naturally we talk about help for Finland. 'What shall we send them?' he asks, 'we have plenty of munitions but we have not yet all the anti-tank weapons, which we should like to have...the airmen talk in the same strain. After all, it is always the same delicate production problem, which hampers us.' Why then did we promise the Finns help that neither we nor the English are capable of giving?

3 *March* 1940. Viborg still holds out. They say that the Boches are advising the Russians who, alone, would never conquer Finland.

General Gamelin came to visit our sector at Valenciennes. He was very pleased and our division was congratulated. General Dame, who was attached to his Staff, and had the honour of being present at his conference, asked him to send our division into camp for further training. Gamelin replied: 'I have massed all the North African and Moroccan divisions on the Belgian frontier, I shall keep them there as long as I have any fears.'

The fifth columnists have been spreading the rumour that Gamelin is in his dotage. It is false, of course. What a modest man he is, he doesn't indulge in speeches and self-advertisement. I like unassuming men, such as Foch, Joffre and Salazar. Compare them with Hitler and Mussolini, the world's two greatest mountebanks.

Influenza

Our football team has played the 92/1 Engineers in vile weather. What a beating we've had: 17 to nil. Never mind, my men enjoyed it, and as we have beaten quite a good number of other teams we are still second in our league—the small units.

5 *March* 1940. I have an attack of 'flu; temperature 104; but am not depressed, and dictate my letters in bed without undue fatigue.

The English have seized some Italian vessels carrying German coal from Rotterdam to Italy. Rome protests noisily, but London stands firm. Berlin applies the bellows to the fire. How will it end?

9 *March* 1940. Finland has sent plenipotentiaries to Moscow. It is the end, and it is a heavy moral defeat for the Allies. I realize this when I talk to the men, who are bewildered by the inactivity of the Allies. I cannot tell them the underlying reasons; I try to minimize the event by showing them help would have meant dispersing our forces. A plausible excuse.

10 *March* 1940. The newspapers announce in great headlines that we are ready to send an expeditionary force of 50,000 men if Helsinki requires it. And how shall we send it, since Sweden and Norway refuse right of way? It's just a sop to public opinion.

12 *March* 1940. Finland has not yet signed, but it is only a matter of hours. We are disheartened.

England has speedily settled the dispute over the seized Italian boats; she has climbed down, letting them all go, save one, retained for form's sake. Berlin interprets this as a sign of weakness.

We are still working hard for the Engineers. I am getting better and am up, but my legs are still shaky.

14 *March* 1940. It's done! Finland has signed, she agrees to be stripped of the Karelian Isthmus, Viborg, Lake Ladoga which gave her protection on the north and Hango, which, in Russian

hands, will threaten Helsinki and the Gulf of Finland. She is bound hand and foot.

On the whole, a complete victory for the Russians and the Germans, an absolute check for the British and ourselves, who gave orders at Geneva to fifty nations to exclude the Russians and to help Finland by all possible means. Who will believe now, after the crushing of Austria, Czecho-Slovakia, Poland, Finland, in the promises of help and protection that we have given? What arguments based on facts can be put forward when we seek to advise neutral states to resist German demands, when neither the British nor ourselves have been able to keep a single promise to send an aeroplane to Poland or a soldier to Finland. What humiliation to be always in tow of the gangsters of Berlin—and perhaps of Rome—who have all the diplomatic, military and moral successes.

How could Sumner Welles fail to be impressed when Hitler said to him: 'The war? It's finished and there will be no more war if the French and English, from whom I claim nothing despite the fact that they have taken my colonies and have no claims on me, consent now to demobilize. Speak to those gentlemen, and not to me.'

16 *March* 1940.   The Senate has had a secret session following the stir caused by the capitulation of Finland. Pierre Laval, they say, has given Daladier a severe jolt. There were many absentees, which means that the Government has many opponents at this critical time. That is to be expected after our blusterings at Geneva, and our passivity towards this heroic little country. The Cabinet is very sick.

Still very hard work for men and horses at Wargnies-le-Grand; I have to send them extra food and fodder to enable them to stand up to it.

17 *March* 1940.   Uneasiness persists in the House, it is rumoured. Daladier is going to reshuffle his Cabinet.

For the last fortnight, our divisional Staff has been working steadily at what it calls 'Plan D' (i.e. Dyle), in case Belgium is violated by the Germans. In agreement with the Belgians, our armies of the North, under the command of our friend General Billotte, would, by seven night marches, take up positions on the Dyle (tributary of the Escaut) in front of Brussels. Our division preceded by a light armoured division and flanked by the Moroccan divisions, would occupy a rather narrow front, therefore compact. Colonel Legrez, our Chief of Staff, has kindly shown me the large-scale maps on which every eventuality is marked by differently coloured hachures: the billets for six days' marching, the positions of each unit, etc. Everything appears to have been carefully thought out. One section of my vehicles will relieve the infantry of their load of blankets and packs, so that the men can march twenty miles daily without undue fatigue.

But will the Boches attack Belgium? While preparing for an attack, most people believe it to be improbable. The population of that country is so dense that they could not divert any food. The speed and the radius of aeroplanes is so great that the space gained to reach England is negligible. If, in 1914, surprise played such a part that the Germans were able to reach the gates of Paris in a few weeks, this time we are on our guard, our system of defence at the frontier, although imperfect, would shelter us if the Germans drove us back, and there they would break their teeth. Above all, to violate the neutrality of Belgium a second time, would arouse the indignation of the whole world, and of the United States in particular. I cannot believe that they will yet again commit this enormous mistake, which, as things are, would bring them untold disappointment.

That doesn't mean to say that our General Staff are in any way wrong in facing up to all possibilities of war. Far from it!

20 *March* 1940. I have just returned from the divisional Staff office. In spite of the paper preparations on the 'Dyle Plan', it is considered that we shall not make a move before July. For the moment, I have the kitchen garden dug and sown with radishes, salads, spinach and carrots. Gamelin forecasts the Belgian campaign and I the summer garden campaign. Will he gather laurels on the Dyle or I radishes in Maing? We'll lay odds.

I foresee no good for us from the interview at the Brenner

Pass between Hitler and Mussolini. The two confederates have not met to buy us a present. Just now they are trying to oust us from the Balkans so as to be able to drain off all their crops, oil and metals.

One wonders, is the blockade of Germany effective? It is more than doubtful, for I have just seen figures proving that the neutrals of Europe have increased their imports to a volume equal to Germany's lost imports. The neutrals then sell their surplus imports to Germany. This was to be expected.

21 *March* 1940.   Daladier has tendered the Cabinet's resignation following the vote taken in secret session, for the noes, together with those who abstained from voting, exceeded the ayes. The socialists have voted against, and a great number of radicals of the Daladier hue have abstained. The moral effect on the troops is bad.

It is said that the Finland affair counts for something in the fall of the Cabinet. Parliament wants also our production, especially of airplanes, to be speedily increased. There seems to be some lack of coordination in the production works. Sometimes we do not get enough propellers, sometimes not enough engines, sometimes not enough planes.

Paul Reynaud has undertaken to form the new Cabinet. Let us wait and see who will form the new team.

The British have reacted quickly to the recent German attack at Scapa Flow; they have bombed the naval air-bases on the island of Sylt for seven solid hours, causing much damage.

22 *March* 1940.   The speed with which the new Cabinet has been formed proves that the conspirators had agreed to overthrow Daladier. The Cabinet is a challenge to common sense and to public opinion.

Sometimes I hear very violent remarks; certain officers, carried away by their will to fight and to fight with all the implements of modern warfare, go so far as to ask for divisions from the front to march on Paris and put a general at the head of a real War Cabinet. The politicians, they say, are responsible for the war (for Hitler would never have dared to do what he

has done if France had been strong), and they permit themselves to govern in the name of France.

It is all the more nauseating because this rottenness, this
political canker, is merely superficial. The heart of France is
what it has always been—clean, honest, brave. I realize this all
the more because through my men I can always place my finger
on what is the true France. All of them, humble folk, country
folk, artisans, workpeople, small business proprietors—how
patriotic, upright and worthy they are in every sense of the word.
And how contemptible are those Deputies who get elected to
serve their own ends, and for what they can get out of the people,
rather than for the sincerity of their political convictions. What
is most remarkable is that the people see a schemer and a thief in
every politician. That is the result of those dreadful and per-
petual police, judicial and financial scandals in which Deputies
and Senators are invariably involved.

Our enemies do not waste their time over parliamentary
manœuvres which are both unintelligible and disconcerting.
Spring is now here, the time of trial is probably at hand and look
what a government we have !

25 March 1940.   Yesterday was Easter Day. Fine football
matches between British and French military teams at the
stadium of Valenciennes. Crowds present. The bands of the
Welsh and Scottish regiments have a well-deserved success with
their precise and rhythmic movements. They give an impression
of calm, of finish, of will-power which reflect the qualities of
Britain. The Highlanders, with their green bag-pipes, short
kilts, dark jackets and bonnets, present a picture of beautifully
blended colours. Our team of dragoons beats the Welsh by one
goal to nil. The 11th Zouaves have a drawn game with the Scots.
To-day the team selected from the division has beaten that of
the Valenciennes Athletic Club by one goal to nil.

Our charming friend Bloch, who left us to take charge of
transport in connection with the French Mission to the British
Army at Auxi-le-Chateau, came and lunched with us to-day.
According to the French officers, the British Army is not yet up
to the mark. The officers' qualifications are moderate. They say

that our captains know more than British colonels and that the troops are not sufficiently hardened, although they work much more than ours. Nothing astonishing in that, an army is not made in six months. But Bloch assures us that the British are determined to continue the struggle as long as may be necessary. They talk of the first round of the war lasting three years. After that, we shall see!

Bloch brings us heaps of cigarettes, corned-beef, gin, whisky, etc., purchased at the well-stocked British canteen. The English officers are first-rate companions. We thought so too. Sometimes a padre, a Catholic chaplain, from a neighbouring division, comes and lunches in our mess. He says, with a laugh, 'I am one of those cursed Jesuits', and being full of life and generosity itself, spends 500 francs on his lunch. He makes us a present of three bottles of whisky (we should have to pay 100 francs a piece), and leaves 100 francs for our poorer soldiers and 100 francs for the cook.

26 *March* 1940.   Paul Reynaud has a majority of one in the Chamber, and has decided to carry on. Perhaps it is better than another change. His ministerial statement is incomprehensibly vague.

A night manœuvre by the 11th Zouaves in which I participate with a part of the company. At the starting-point, where all the regiment has to march past at a given time, I meet General Dame and his Staff. The soldiers, relieved of their packs, which are carried on the transport wagons, march by briskly and alertly in files, one on each side of the road. Each battalion takes 12 to 14 minutes to pass accompanied by their lovely police-dogs leashed in pairs and so intelligent looking. The dogs have daily training in message carrying from point to point. After the infantry come a group of the 40th Artillery, half French, half Algerian. They also have their liaison dogs, which they carry in travelling cages.

Behind these come the Anti-Tank Defence Battalion, with their very modern-looking guns, low mounted on rubber tyres. The battalion commander, Captain Marcel, has just returned from the camp at Mailly, where the gun-layers have shown

themselves to be first-class with 96 per cent of the shells on the
mark; five out of six reached 100 per cent on moving targets.
This is thanks to the daily training which they undergo in all
weathers and over all types of ground. If all commanding
officers are like him, what splendid results we will get ! The new
guns at 1200 yards range will penetrate three normal plates of
German tank armour spaced an inch or so apart. If the army
had these guns in sufficient numbers, Marcel told me, not a
single tank could reach our lines.

At 1 a.m. on a cold and inky-black night, accompanied by
squalls of rain, collar turned up and head buried in my great-
coat, I make for Maing by tracks over a great heath that I had
crossed only once before. Not a tree, not a house, no landmark.
Shall I find my way? I drop the reins on my mare's neck, she is
so intelligent. At cross-roads she noses to the right, then to the
left, and goes off without hesitation. But once I had the feeling
that she had taken the wrong path. I stopped and read my map,
with the aid of a torch. She is right. In front of the stable, she
stops, and to test her, I endeavour to make her go on again, but
she turns her head, as if to say, 'Stupid, don't you realize that we
are home'. The stable orderly is so sound asleep that I haven't
the heart to wake him up. I unsaddle my mare, wisp her down
and rub her back where the saddle has been. Her hay and oats
are ready; just as I am about to leave her, the affectionate
animal rubs her muzzle against my face as if to kiss me and say
good-night.

During this long solitary journey, the scene was grand and
awe-inspiring, immense and bare, the heath stretching away
into the distance with no sign of life, not even the barking of a
dog. In the distance the blast furnaces of the North-Eastern
Ironworks at Valenciennes, when tapped, release streams of
molten metal and fantastic showers of sparks light up the low-
hanging clouds like a volcano in eruption. The whole sky reddens,
suddenly lighting up the desolate countryside, where beneath
the storm writhe the skeletons of a few stunted trees in their
winter garb. Alone, feeling so small and puny, with my mare as
sole companion, as she keeps her head to the ground to find the
way, I feel a sensuous joy in my solitude; it is as if I belonged

to a lost age, an age when men had to struggle against the unleashed forces of nature; then I remember with delight that a bed, a warm room, aglow with light, await me.

27 *March* 1940.   At 2 p.m. entraining exercise of the divisional headquarters and at 5.30 p.m. night exercise with the 13th Algerian Rifles, the same as carried out yesterday with the 11th Zouaves.

28 *March* 1940.   Mussolini has received Count Teleki, President of the Hungarian Cabinet.   Much ado in the Balkans, but not to our advantage.

29 *March* 1940.   Another night exercise, this time with the 22nd Algerian Rifles.   Desouches is put in command of part of a supply detachment which Colonel Dubost has the bright idea of placing under the orders of the regimental veterinary officer. Result: the worthy Vet. gets lost, and goes off in the wrong direction. The poor weary foot-sloggers march 8 miles extra and everybody is in a vile temper.

30 *March* 1940.   Paul Reynaud feels the need to do something to strengthen his tottering position.   He has sent home Souritz, the Soviet Ambassador, on the grounds that he has sent an open telegram to Stalin on the occasion of the Peace with Finland, and that this is prejudicial to Great Britain and to us.
To-day, at the Supreme War Council in London, he has signed with Chamberlain a solemn declaration of Franco-British unity of action during and after the war. This solemn, mutual engagement is excellent in my opinion; we have never been so united with our Ally, whose war aims are identical with ours. During hostilities, we shall always be in agreement; it is after the victory that we must remain united and neither of us must fall into the same faults as we did in 1919.

31 *March* 1940.   The Franco-British declaration of indissoluble unity has created a favourable impression in neutral countries, so the newspapers report.   Paul Reynaud is lucky, he

remains in office because both Chambers have taken a few days'
holiday for Easter. Reynaud, Mandel, and a few others inspire
me with confidence, but the rest are undesirables.

3 *April* 1940.   Off on my second leave to my dear Ghislaine at
Toulon.

9 *April* 1940.   Toulon. The Germans have invaded Norway,
excusing themselves with the grotesque lie that they were
merely forestalling us. At nine o'clock in the evening, while we
are having a hand of bridge with some naval officers, an urgent
telegram arrives, recalling me. I had been expecting it all day.
The naval officers think that Britain has set a trap for Germany,
in order to entice her fleet from its lair and thus have a chance of
smashing it.

12 *April* 1940.   The Germans have suffered the expected
heavy naval defeat. The British have landed troops in Norway
who resist as best they can, pending the arrival of our reinforcements.

14 *April* 1940.   We are in a state of emergency. It was feared
yesterday that the Germans would attack Belgium, with thirty-
five divisions, so I understand from the Intelligence. Rumours?
Or have the Germans, because of their check in Norway and the
prospect of a long and difficult campaign in Scandinavia, abandoned this attempt? For, once we are at grips in Belgium, there
will be no breathing-space as in 1914–18. I keep my men standing by in billets, ready to harness up, for we have to move off,
one hour after zero, for Vicoigne, to the north of Valenciennes,
where the division is due to concentrate. I have seen our proposed billets.

15 *April* 1940.   An officer of the Army Staff at divisional
Headquarters assures us that the French and British ambassadors have asked Brussels for permission to enter Belgium in
order to attack the Germans, or at least to reinforce the Belgian
Army along the line of its fortifications. Belgium refuses,

wishing, even if Holland is attacked, to maintain its chance of neutrality to the end. What risk does she run? She knows that in any case we shall go to her help with our armies massed on her frontier. Her reasons may be clever, but they are neither moral nor praiseworthy and are probably dangerous, for we shall be two or three days behind the Germans, a delay terribly risky and ominous.

At half-past seven each evening we listen to the French broadcast from Rome, more violent, and if possible more anti-French than Berlin itself. One would laugh at it, were it not an indication of criminal intentions. According to the Italians, the British and ourselves have violated Norwegian neutrality, and thanks be to God, the Germans are there to protect the poor little nations threatened and tortured by us. Of course, we have no successes in Norway, but are meeting with bloody defeats.

17 *April* 1940.   The British are very sporting, they announce freely the loss of some ships and ten planes. Their sincerity inspires confidence.

I think that once again we shall have to give up the idea of entering Belgium. What a disappointment! Our men, like those of the infantry regiments, are itching to march. General Dame orders me to unload and resume light jobs immediately around the billets.

We are more and more worried over the Balkans, where the Italians are concentrating troops in Albania as a jumping off point for Salonika and the road to the Bosphorus.

The British seem to be completely masters of Narvik, whence the Germans flee to reach Sweden, where they are disarmed. This source of iron supply is definitely cut off from the Germans, and without that iron they cannot cast guns or shells. Mr Chamberlain is probably right when he states that the war has been shortened by two years. Contact has been established with the Norwegian troops, but the Germans hold the lines of communication to Oslo and can quickly reinforce their troops.

I learn at Headquarters that two of our Alpine divisions are en route for Norway. The Germans declare that they have nothing to fear so long as there are only the British in front of them, but with our mountain troops they'll change their tune.

18 *April* 1940.   Our horses feed every day on the grass of the banks, their winter coats have fallen, their bodies are fat and sleek. The men polish and furbish the metal parts, grease the harness and vehicles. Everything is spick and span.

At Headquarters the chances of Italy entering the war against us are hotly discussed. Weygand in Syria is being reinforced. If we don't enter Belgium, perhaps we shall find ourselves on the Bosphorus, anywhere rather than do nothing.

19 *April* 1940.   From my window this morning I have seen the first swallows skimming over the luscious grass of tender green that covers the long, gently sloping meadow. Fine black and white cattle graze there.

As expected, the state of emergency is now ended, save for a few precautions necessary to speed up any future departure. My sections remain with the Infantry regiments, ready to load up. To-morrow we shall resume work in the fields to the great delight of the farmers, impatient to get on with the sowing of oats, and ploughing for the beet.

21 *April* 1940.   Beautiful weather, 95 degrees in the sun. We lunch beneath the arbour in the garden which, without its leaves, still looks like a great cluster of twigs. We eat the first radishes from the garden. Desouches and I have had a lovely ride along the Escaut, through little copses of tender green foliage.

22 *April* 1940.   A great shock for me. I am one of a dozen officers who, being more than forty years old, are to be sent home to command labour units. At my request, General Dame and Colonel Legrez, Chief of Staff, put in a word on my behalf to General Blanchard, Commander of the 1st Army. I am allowed to remain with the North African Division, which I wouldn't leave at any cost. My friends who have to go are very jealous. I express my great gratitude to General Dame and to the Colonel. They say very nice things about me. How heart-breaking it

would have been to leave my brave poilus of whom I am so fond, and who are, I believe, equally fond of me.

Lieutenant Fere of the Intelligence tells me that our expeditionary corps has landed at four points near Trondheim, where the Germans' position will be considerably threatened.

25 *April* 1940. The communiqués from Norway are disquieting. Heavy material must obviously be landed, and this is a difficult operation, as we have only small ports with poor facilities at our disposal, while the Germans hold all the big ports—Oslo, Bergen, Trondheim—where night and day they can land a hundred times more supplies and troops. Further, they are the masters of the main lines of communication. We have nothing like it. Does the studied vagueness of the communiqués hide a more difficult situation than was at first supposed?

27 *April* 1940. The blockade of Norway is not effective. German boats have landed six to eight fresh divisions with supplies at Oslo. Advancing by rail, these 150,000 men will soon bring their weight to bear on our expeditionary force to the south of Trondheim, which will be attacked from the north and south, for the Germans, advancing by forced marches, have driven from their positions the few Norwegian troops who attempted to block the way from Oslo to Trondheim.

We have resumed our half barrack, half waiting-for-war style of life. Lieutenant Jans is on leave. I stay with the M.O. and the Vet.

29 *April* 1940. At the Officers' conference, Captain de Lambert of 'Operations' gives us a talk on operations in Norway, showing us the respective positions of the armies on an immense map. It is evident that our little expeditionary force is going to be caught to the south of Trondheim, between the German forces coming from the north and the south, if the two German corps meet in the region of Dombas.

Narvik, contrary to what had been announced, is not entirely in British hands. Why give us such high hopes?

Flame-throwers

General Dame refrains from all comment, merely saying, 'Clearly, as long as we are inferior on land to the Germans, the situation will remain difficult'. What does he mean? Does he refer only to Norway or the whole situation?

According to de Lambert, the Intelligence have information that the Germans have built a number of motor-driven barges of 700 tons, capable of navigation on the Rhine and the Escaut; they can hold 450 men and their equipment. Everything seems to indicate that they are preparing to invade Holland at no distant date.

Another item of news; on the Eastern front, one of our outposts was attacked by a detachment of 60 men, armed with heavy machine-guns and commanded by a sergeant-major. The first Verey light gave the signal for their trench mortars to open fire and a second flare brought down a box barrage. The sergeant-major was killed, however, and the attack beaten off. On picking up his body, we found that he carried a flame-thrower. That is worth while knowing. Why are we squeamish about employing the same barbaric weapons?

30 *April* 1940.   The General advises us to look after the morale of our men; we must give them some distraction. The postal censorship shows that the men are fed up, as they do not understand this life of dormant war in which they have the impression of being useless, while their fields or their businesses call them.

I have organized a little jollification in our club (now called 'Café Maure' so as to escape the new and ridiculous regulation which brings all soldiers' clubs under the control of the ladies of the Red Cross).   Our scratch orchestra consists of two fiddles, a saxophone (excellent), a banjo with vocal accompaniment, and two little local girls who have kindly given their help—good heavens, their singing is awful—and the party is in full swing. Choruses and songs!   I have the bright idea of a dancing competition: couples in heavy military boots take the floor.   One after another, very seriously, they perform a tango, a waltz and a rumba. The jury, over which I preside, awards the 1st, 2nd and 3rd prizes, consisting of bottles of champagne (if one may call it

so) or of Bordeaux. My poilus have a hectic time and we have a
good laugh. Next time, we shall be able to improve on it.

1 *May* 1940.   The Germans have joined forces at Dombas and
claim that they are in pursuit. Our communiqué speaks only of
heavy pressure forcing us to retire to the north of the town. I
don't like the tone of it.

2 *May* 1940.   It is admitted that our troops to the south
of Trondheim have had to re-embark and that the operation
has been carried out 'with complete success'. A marvellous
euphemism! We saw it coming several days ago.

3 *May* 1940.   Again 'with complete success' our troops which
had landed at Namsos, to the north of Trondheim, have also
re-embarked. We hold on only in the region of Narvik, in the
extreme north. For how long? What material and moral success for the Germans! What a new blow to us in the eyes of the
neutrals! Sweden imprisoned between Finland and Norway
falls, *ipso facto*, at least economically, into the hands of the
Germans. What increase of resources for them.

We shall have the initiative in operations only when the
British have been able to enrol, equip and above all train two or
three million men. I cannot, without sadness, think of the last
war when it took them three years to put on foot an army which
never equalled ours, probably for want of officers and N.C.O.s.
The answer I receive is always: 'That is so. The English have no
army, but they have a navy, and what a navy! You can't have
everything.' Why? Cannot a rich old lady afford both a foot-
man and a chauffeur?

4 *May* 1940.   Italy is very threatening. The British already
send some of their merchant ships round the Cape of Good Hope
instead of through the Mediterranean. This Italian menace is
probably one of the causes of the abandonment of Norway, the
number of warships sent to the Mediterranean preventing an
efficient blockade of the Scandinavian coast. The Japanese
threaten to 'take under their protection' the Dutch East Indies,

their commercial *Lebensraum*, if Holland is invaded by Germany. Doubtless to 'protect' it, in the Boche manner. America protests, saying she will not remain inactive. Bravo! But with what army will she intervene? It is always the same, how many years will she take to build up this army and what will it be worth?

The plan of three great birds of prey becomes daily clearer. Soldiers returning from leave in Paris state that the Norwegian check has caused a considerable lowering of morale on the home front. The public is wrong; remember the 1914–18 war, in which for three and a half years we had nothing but checks, except at the Marne and Verdun, and they, after all, were only delaying actions. Our offensive began on 18 July 1918 and the Germans signed the Armistice on 11 November.

9 May 1940.   Lunch with the General; the talk is merely about organizing our local summer and winter activities. The chaplain of Headquarters and another officer hurry over their meals, they are going on leave. The General teases them, for twice already they have been recalled by telegram; but this time, he thinks, it will be uninterrupted.

This evening, dinner in the mess with a dozen friends from the divisional Staff. Lobster à l'américaine, truffled fowl, etc. I play bridge until one o'clock in the morning with Captain Perrier, Chief of the Operational Staff, Captain Fumey, Chief of the Supply Staff, Major Lauzeral, Chief of the Army Medical Corps. Then we go peacefully to bed. A rendezvous has been arranged for dinner in their mess, next week.

10 May 1940.   I am awakened about 3 a.m. by the incessant noise of waves of planes passing over the house, but I am tired and soon sleep again.

At eight o'clock I receive the order to stand by. Contrary to all the forecasts of the British and French Staffs, who apparently knew nothing, the Germans have invaded Holland and Belgium. During the night, when we had barely finished our bridge party, they heavily bombed all our aerodromes in the north, and the east, as far as Le Bourget. It is done and the die is cast, but once again we have been forestalled and caught napping.

I hastily send forward to the Infantry regiments the light vehicles, forage wagons, etc. ready to transport kits, blankets and packs. At 4.30 p.m., driving through Valenciennes with Lieutenant Rougetet of the Ordnance Corps, we pass, near the station, a heap of rubble which had been a house 30 seconds earlier, now destroyed by a couple of bombs. A car, which was passing at the time of the explosion, was hurled by the blast into the interior of the house just as it collapsed. The car was buried upside down beneath the rubbish, only two burst tyres could be seen and a part of the back. An enormous flame of gas spurted from the broken roadway.

Later a damaged German bomber fell in the town and its bombs exploded.

An hour later we pass by again. Life in Valenciennes has not been interrupted for one minute, no sign of fright, nor even of nerves. At eight o'clock I leave with the last sections of my company. Many feminine tears are shed for us after these four months spent in Maing. Our men are full of life and cheerfulness.

We arrive at Raismes-Vicoigne at 1 a.m. At 2 a.m. we start off again to take up our positions near the frontier, arriving at 7 a.m.

11 *May* 1940.　We enter Belgium at Bonsecours and sleep at Grandglise at the charming chateau of M. Pollet, who is kindness itself. Everywhere the welcome is most cordial, the French soldiers inspire absolute confidence. Many cars full of refugees from the Liège region are racing towards France. The news these people bring is pessimistic. Is that because they wish to justify their flight? Treachery and the fifth column are the sole topics of conversation. We listen, but we remain rather sceptical and not a little amused. M. Pollet gives us cause to reflect when he tells us of the political manœuvrings by which Walloons have been ousted from the King's Staff and the General Army Staff, and replaced by definitely germanophil Flemings.

12 *May* 1940.　We sleep at Bolignies, a little hamlet near Brugelette at the house of a former burgomaster, a nice old

fellow. Countless fantastic yarns go round about the fall of the forts of Liège; the Germans are supposed to have crossed the Albert canal and the great south-eastern line of defence; they are supposed to be already in Tirlemont. It is unbelievable! These reports can only have been spread by spies, who are everywhere and have been dropped by parachute.

13 *May* 1940.   Few German planes in the sky; a solitary flier has machine-gunned the main entrance of the chateau de Cambron-Casteau. We go and examine a Heinkel brought down on the Lombise road by British fighters; this bomber, still carrying two or three incendiary bombs, was returning from a small raid on Nancy. It is riddled with bullets and stained with the blood of two of the crew who had been killed. The pilot was taken prisoner.

Few French planes in the air, but a good number of British and Canadian Curtiss machines with one white and one black wing.

The bad news from the front can be read in the look of anguish of the civilians as they watch us pass. The women are bent, and stand there weeping, their hands clasped over their aching bodies.

We sleep at Steenkerque, on the very spot where the battle of that name was fought. We reach this green-wooded and hilly region by terrible, narrow, cobbled roads. They are in such a dreadful condition that they would be considered a scandal in France.

14 *May* 1940.   This morning at six o'clock Steenkerque had its first bombing; a dozen bombs were dropped, without any result, from machines going over slowly at a low altitude. Our fighter planes must have been elsewhere, for none came to mar the Boches' little outing. No newspapers; but the radio announces that Holland is invaded and that Rotterdam is in flames. The Dutch Government has taken refuge in England after three days' fighting. Fortunately our poilus have no more idea where Rotterdam is than Pekin, so this news does not worry them. They say that so long as the Boches have to deal with the

Belgians and the Dutch anything may happen, but when they meet our army, the party will soon be over.

The communiqués concerning operations in Belgium are, alas, very vague; only 'heavy pressure' and 'strategic withdrawal' are mentioned, no one dares give the extreme points of the German advance; they have also attacked the French frontier near Longwy. The situation appears to be very serious.

The mayor's secretary, in a great state of excitement, came to fetch me to arrest a spy disguised as a soldier. After inquiries, I find that it was a lad of the neighbourhood talking to one of our men.

Wonderful weather—quiet and lovely.

15 *May* 1940. We reach Haut-Ittre, in the direction of the Dyle, by very hilly roads which necessitate double teams of horses. The number of refugees on foot, in farm-carts, and cars, increases from hour to hour; they jam all roads and prevent the movement of military convoys. What are the army traffic control doing? They are conspicuous by their absence; the routes to be followed by fast convoys, heavy convoys, and one-way traffic are not specified. Everywhere traffic-blocks! In 1917 this service worked perfectly. Have we unlearnt the lessons of the last war?

The terrifying advance of the Germans has forced us to hasten our movements. The division has been transported by lorry to the Dyle; but certain units have not followed on, and have arrived late on account of the congestion on the roads due to lack of traffic control and to the crowds of refugees who ought to have been stopped at all cost. Generally speaking, the General Staff have transformed J 7 into J 4, that is, we are required to take up our positions on the Dyle on the fourth day of the offensive instead of the seventh day. So we have lost three days for preparing our position, as the Belgians gave ground on the first day instead of holding out for seven days.

Heavy bombing from the air, two men slightly wounded, three horses killed and five wounded. Our fighters must be some miles ahead at the front, for we do not see a single machine in the sky.

At 3 p.m. a summons to Headquarters, which functions from a little country-house not far from the monument of Waterloo. Sad omen! General Dame puts me in command of all the divisional ambulances, the heavy engineers, the pioneers and the headquarter company of the 22nd Regiment (I could not find the latter, they had camped in a wood away from the rest, but rejoined us later during the night). He orders me to retreat as far as Maing, which we left five days ago, and broadly speaking I am to save everything possible by requisitioning horses and refugees' cars if necessary. My column will stretch from 5 to 7 miles along the road and will include eight to nine hundred horses and 1500 men. Headquarters seems to be very alarmed; our regiments in contact with the Germans during the last two days held until this morning; then the front, on our right, showed signs of cracking under the weight of German motorized columns. The men's resistance was heroic; I think that Gamelin gave the order to hold at all costs. Men let themselves be crushed by the tanks rather than give way. The losses must be heavy. There was no shortage of ammunition, but the number of tanks was insufficient. They sometimes fought one against ten, and ploughed their way through the Boches. But their losses are already terrible. Contrary to their pledged word, the Belgians had prepared no positions. Not a single position was prepared, not a trench dug, not a yard of barbed wire run. They were supposed to hold the Albert canal for seven days, so that we could organize our positions on the Dyle. They didn't hold six hours, nor even blow up the bridges. Everywhere Belgian troops retire in confusion. The battle of the Dyle is lost. We are falling back behind the fortifications that we have just constructed on the frontier which, together with the fortified sector of the Escaut, are manned by divisions brought up from the rear.

16 *May* 1940. Arrive at 7 a.m. at Graty-Boscante. We are bombed and machine-gunned several times between 4 and 6 p.m. Our machine-guns fired 3000 rounds at the planes without any visible results. Few casualties on the whole in my column, which has collected all stragglers and small details on the way; no real damage done. Our air force must be occupied in delaying the

enemy's advance, for we never see any sign of it. I have com-
mandeered twenty-seven magnificent horses; anything we leave
behind will be of use to the enemy.

The Staff of the Army Corps had to move quickly to avoid
capture. It is reported that units had difficulty in passing
through Nivelles, which was in flames. There are rumours as to
the losses in the infantry regiments of the division which held
their ground to the last, crushed by tanks, bombed and machine-
gunned by enemy planes. Heavy losses among the officers, who
were splendid, as was to be expected. We must have lost 30 per
cent of our guns and enormous supplies of ammunition.

The men want to know where I am leading them, but I conceal
the fact that we are returning to France. They feel that things
are not going too well, but do not suspect defeat.

17 *May* 1940.   Arrived at Neufmaison at 6 a.m. We are not
attacked from the air. Departure at 10 p.m.

18 *May* 1940.   We cross the frontier again at Bonsecours at
dawn. Ugh! What a relief! There at least, behind our defences,
we can breathe.

But refugees, fleeing towards the interior of France, tell us
that our pill-boxes are unoccupied. During a long halt, giving
my mare a chance to rest, I gallop forward on another horse and
am astonished to find our blockhouses empty. Why did the
High Command adopt these tactics? This beats me!

We pass through Valenciennes, which has suffered considerably from German bombs. After leaving Trith St Leger,
a squadron of twenty-seven Messerschmitts flies over us steadily
at a height of 700 feet, without changing course.

The Vet.'s nerves are all on edge, so are mine, expecting a
catastrophe at any moment. If we are attacked it will be a
shambles. I ride up and down the column to encourage the men
who, silent and with set jaws, never wince. There is perfect order
everywhere.

Arrive at Maing at midday; it is nearly deserted. We unhar-
ness and each one returns to his old billet. The Messerschmitts

decide to attack us with bombs and machine-guns. The men make for the shelters. No damage done. But I learn that the Germans have penetrated the frontier in the neighbourhood of Maubeuge and are now less than 20 miles from Maing. I understand why the fortifications have not been manned. The Germans who have made a break through the frontier would have gone round them. I send the Vet. to reconnoitre by car; I leave Jans in command and return with the M.O. commanding the ambulance corps in a motor ambulance to Vicoigne to get orders. Impossible to find the divisional Headquarters, but they are said to be making for Saint Amand.

On returning to Maing, I lighten my vehicles of all unnecessary gear and we retrace our steps in a northerly direction. Our horses will have covered 50 miles before nightfall, but they are going strong.

19 *May* 1940.   Our divisional Staff is installed in the town hall of Saint Amand. The town has suffered considerably and few houses remain intact. Less than fifty civilians remain and the troops are allowed to take from the houses anything they need, for we know that the Germans will be here within a few days. The officers can dip into the cellars of the Hotel de Paris, on the Place du Beffroi, to their heart's content; a sentry stands at the door and only officers are allowed to enter. More than ten thousand bottles of the best vintages are taken away. I load up Desouches' Simca, which he has given me, with fifty miscellaneous bottles: Burgundy, Bordeaux, Champagne. We take up our billets in a forester's house in Flines Wood; the men sleep in their vehicles. A Canadian Curtiss attacks three Messerschmitts, brings down two in less than three minutes and puts the third to flight. Instantly our men are bucked up like hell, and their spirits rise. Actually, they had been bewildered rather than discouraged. There is nothing much wrong with them. In the evening we move our billets 4 miles to Beuvry Nord, south of Orchies, to an abandoned farm, on a sort of island, surrounded by water and small woods. We did well to move, for an hour later the square patch of wood where we were stationed was violently bombed from the air.

British anti-aircraft

20 *May* 1940.   The first day of rest. We take advantage of it to lay in a stock of fodder from the neighbouring evacuated farms.

The convoys of refugees are much less numerous. On the main road from Saint Amand to Lille, many of these poor folks have fallen victims to Hitler's bombs. Around a single crater I counted eighteen women and children killed.

A British anti-aircraft battery, in position a few hundred yards from us, is doing fine work; two planes down this morning before breakfast. The Germans now avoid it carefully and we are left in peace all day. Our anti-aircraft batteries cannot be compared with the British, which are more efficient than ours. Their firing is much better grouped and more accurate.

Lieutenant Ferry of the Motor Transport temporarily attached to Headquarters assures me that he has seen the plans for defence, first on the line of the Escaut, then on the forest of Raismes and finally on the Scarpe. The losses in Belgium are probably less than was at first thought. General Dame, whom all staff officers, without exception, reckon as a great 'ace', and which doesn't surprise me, affirms that if he had had one regiment and an anti-tank battalion more in the place of the 32nd Infantry Division, which gave way on his right, he would still be on the Dyle.

21 *May* 1940.   The General entrusts to me the job of providing a cattle-park in case provisions run short. I advise against it; how can one keep water, and feed a large quantity of horned cattle? It is better to let them wander in small groups, as they do now; he agrees.

The general feeling is better. Our army corps, supported by Maulde Fort, has repulsed heavy German attacks. This Fort is the pivot of the forward line of resistance on the frontier.

But the fifth column really does exist; every night blue, green and red lights appear everywhere. A regiment cannot remain two hours in a tiny spot without being invariably bombed with enormous bombs, the smoke of which rises in the sky to the height of some 300 feet. The regiment moves on and the bombing ceases.

Gamelin superseded

Much movement of troops taking up their positions; this evening a battalion of light infantry and a regiment of Zouaves have moved up. It is the third time in five days that the Zouaves, very proud and full of hope, have taken up battle positions. At half-past nine the bugles in the village and copse sound 'lights out'; the night is cloudless and peaceful. The Zouaves, supple and strong, march on in silence, covered with dust.

22 May 1940.   Our orders are to shoot all spies and strangers who are unable to justify their presence in the zone; also those who give orders to retire or start panicking. No fuss or bother, merely keep an account of the total number dealt with.

23 May 1940.   Set out at 10 p.m. for Le Riez, a little to the north and nearer Orchies. I am able to disperse and conceal my men in vast orchards. Immediately on arriving now, the men seize picks and shovels and rapidly dig shelter-trenches.

No news; no newspapers; no wireless, as there is no electricity in the region, but am afraid that Pétain has become Prime Minister with Daladier still at the War Office. Mandel is at the Home Office, Gamelin has been superseded! What a disappointment in this man! Weygand has taken his place; he surely will pull us through.

The front seems stable on our side, the men live like fighting cocks: chickens, pork, mutton, drinks. We have orders to make use of the local resources and we do so generously.

But a rumour, which two days ago I had dismissed with a shrug, is confirmed; the Germans, having entered France by Stenay, Maubeuge, etc., are now at Boulogne-sur-Mer and Calais. So we are encircled! It's flabbergasting! Shall we succeed in breaking through the circle or shall we be taken prisoner? The whole of the North of France, Belgium, our lines of fortifications, our immense quantities of material, hundreds of thousands of men, thanks to this manœuvre of unexampled audacity, are perhaps about to fall into the hands of the Boches. The Army is now aware of it, but it is in no wise discouraged. All the same, what a disaster! I realize now why those small forts were unoccupied. The enemy having turned the position from the south, they were of no further use.

25 *May* 1940. Main direction of retirement: Dunkirk, where an effort will be made to embark the French, British, and Belgian Armies. We move 15 to 25 miles nightly. The division is regrouped as army reserve in the Mons-en-Pevelle sector. My orders are to proceed with my troops to Houpelin.

26 *May* 1940. An army under the command of General Frère is marching northwards to meet us near Bapaume. We shall attack from the north, in a southerly direction. There is heavy gunfire to the south. Our division, which faced Belgium, has hastily swung round to face south. Our fine regiments, which at the outset had 3000 men, now have only 1300 after the Dyle and Maulde Fort engagements. All the same, they attack with great courage. Heavy losses among the officers, who always lead. There is a report this evening that the attack has been successful and that the Germans have been cut off. All their advanced units between Bapaume and the sea will fall into our hands. That shows the Weygand touch! The German manœuvre will end disastrously. We dance for joy.

Heavy bombing this evening on all our billets. A few men are wounded, a few horses killed. Our old Saint-Etienne machine-guns let fly a thousand rounds. I receive orders to take my unit to Wattignies to-night.

27 *May* 1940. Alas! all the information was false. Frère's army had no other mission than to obstruct the formidable German advance towards the south. The High Command appears to have given up hope of saving us. We must reach Dunkirk at all costs.

I am ordered to billet in a wood on the other side of the Lys. Just as we are about to enter the wood, a liaison car comes up to me. The wood is already partly occupied by the Germans. We have to turn about and retrace our steps. Twenty-seven planes give us a warm quarter of an hour, an orgy of dive-bombing, looping the loop, aerobatics which fill us with rage. No A.A., not a single fighter, French or British. What can we do with our old Saint-Etienne instructional machine-guns, worn out, and with an enormous amount of play in the mechanism? The Germans return three times to the attack, in absolute safety. In my unit, one man killed, a few wounded, three horses killed, ten or a dozen wounded. But in other units of the column the losses are more serious—eleven killed.

Shortly afterwards I came across three tanks commanded by a captain, all that was left of the half brigade of eighty-eight tanks attached to our army corps. In the first engagement they were reduced to fifteen. The fifteen attacked, they became nine. They attacked again and now there are three, but still going strong. They are going to take up their position to defend a crossing. Fine fellows! Every time they have fought at odds varying from four up to ten to one. At two to one, the captain says, we should have had the Boches as easily as winking. But four to one, what can you do?

It is reported that the King of the Belgians has capitulated with all his army, thus exposing the whole flank of the French Army. And he is the son of the Roi-Chevalier. It's the end of everything. It's time we were at Dunkirk.

29 *May* 1940. I billet at Erquinghem on the north bank of the Lys, but no divisional orders come to me. I decide in the evening to go to Steenwerek, where the 1st Army Staff, that is to say ours, is quartered. All contact with our North African Division is lost and no orders come through. The exhausted staff officers are rolled up in blankets and sleep on the floor. Those on duty seem depressed. I hear orders given by 'phone to send a few scattered units still holding out to act as stop-gaps and to try to delay, for an hour or two, the closing-in of the infernal circle and so give time to the others to reach Dunkirk. These unlucky troops attack and counter-attack like maniacs and give their lives like heroes. The regiments melt away visibly; our division has received orders to hold out at all costs. The 13th Rifles attacked again yesterday near Houplines—their sixth attack in eight days. They have only 500 men left, nearly all the officers have been killed, but the N.C.O.s carry on and their spirits

never falter. The 22nd Rifles tell the same story. With only 700 men left, they are ordered to attack again to-night. While I am there, a staff-officer telephones instructions to the General in command at Lille to fire all petrol dumps and blow up the electric power station as the Germans are expected to enter the town to-night.

The roads are congested by convoys. Thanks to indescribable efforts, the Vet. and I, worn out, manage to rejoin the column at midnight. Without awaiting orders, I decide to make for Poperinghe and Dunkirk. Half a mile from Nieppe, there is a frightful traffic jam. All the village streets are blocked. There are eight or ten lines of traffic: horse-drawn vehicles, guns, motor machine-guns, lorries, ambulances, cars full of refugees; so much so that it took just four hours to cover half a mile. German tanks passed at the head of the great jam, firing a few machine-gun belts, then they disappeared. That increased the confusion. At last, towards six o'clock in the morning, we begin to move at a faster pace. I decide to branch off at Neuve Eglise to avoid Poperinghe, which is stated to be under enemy fire.

Large British and French convoys are making for Neuve Eglise, where a counter-attack is being prepared in an attempt to check the advance. British infantry and fifty to sixty British tanks are there in perfect order, so too are French artillery, 155's. Two infantry battalions are mere skeletons. The men look tired, but laugh and joke. They are by no means demoralized. The German planes have quickly located them, and spray all troop concentrations abundantly. On our side, still no aeroplanes in the sky, not even a reconnaissance machine. We fight blindly against an adversary with a hundred eyes, and ten times superior. We climb a slope, and I see the counter-attack developing. The British tanks, very cleverly creeping forward under cover, make a rapid advance. We increase our pace, St Jans Cappel is impracticable, the road having been cut by bombs. Our only way is through a gap of a dozen miles, along which we dodge from side to side over dirt tracks. On arriving at the foot of Mont Noir there is a fresh traffic-block, a mile long, leading to the entrance of Westoutre, where the British have barricaded all exits so that their columns can pass through with greater ease. The French are wild. Some gunners talk of training their guns on them and shooting. As the senior officer present I take command and order two artillery officers to take a hundred men and drag away the heavy British tractors which bar the road. Then I go and find an English major, and in five minutes everything is arranged; they will march off along the Poperinghe road, and the French along the Berguen and Westoutre road. We place a cordon of British and French troops at intervals to mark the route and avoid confusion. The Mont Noir road is cleared of troops in four hours' time and the columns flow smoothly. We must make up for lost time. We march until nine o'clock in the evening, then we halt for two hours so that men and horses may eat and drink. On once more. We have been pressing forward for twenty-one hours without unharnessing.

At break of day, we find ourselves a dozen miles from Dunkirk. The traffic congestion and disorder on the road are indescribable, because the High Command has omitted to organize traffic control through either staff officers, military police or mobile guards. All kinds of arms are there in unparalleled confusion, but our men do not show the slightest sign of panic. They are calm and do their best to clear the way for their vehicles, in spite of the intermittent firing of the German artillery, which destroys quite a bit of their material. A lot of damaged guns, ambulance vans and motor-cars are thrown into the ditches, in order to relieve the congestion on the road. There they are left together with broken equipment and rifles. After unspeakable efforts, we manage to bring our vehicles more or less in order through this retreating maze, the like of which has never been seen before.

The British police the entrance to Bergues; the French have to take the right-hand bank of the canal, the British the left. Hardly have we turned into our road, when we are caught by fairly intense artillery fire. I manage to control my mare, despite the whirlwind flight of four or five hundred horses and mules abandoned in a field, which dash in and out of our teams thereby increasing the confusion. One of the wagons, whose two horses have stampeded, is thrown against me, violently knocks me down, and my mare too; she gets up and bolts off with the other runaways. But the following team, moving fast, is nearly on top of me: I am in danger of being trampled upon and crushed to death. The two drivers strain every limb and manage to slow down, I creep to one side, on all fours, just in time to let the team go by. The Veterinary Surgeon, who was on this cart, jumps down, white with fear on my account. In front of us, one of our wagons, with both horses bolting, plunges into the canal and disappears.

The Vet. and I continue on foot, always under an ever-lengthening artillery fire. Every hundred yards we fall flat down in the ditches, now full of water, as the inundation of the plain is beginning. Down we go, head and all, for dear life's sake. The road is strewn with dead and hundreds of wounded who call for help. What can we do for them? At some distance we see a soldier who appears to be quietly sitting in the road, leaning on a sack; the unfortunate fellow has had half his head blown away— a body crowned with an awful mass of mangled flesh.

We rest for a few moments in a little house where some wounded have taken refuge; an English soldier is vomiting blood, others are improvising dressings for each other's wounds. I promise them an ambulance, to comfort them, but where or how? One of them has a jar of rum, we all have a drink, and the Vet. and I leave.

After six miles of tramping, we arrive at Bray-Dunes. There also the confusion is unbelievable; with difficulty one dodges between thousands of lorries and vehicles abandoned by English and French units already embarked. By chance we come across Desouches and the Ambulance Corps doctors. They tell me that the division is being re-formed on the Belgian frontier, in the dunes near La Panne. We get there by walking down the railway track. From the top of the dunes we overlook the plain where the water slowly mounts and we see the heart-rending sight of tens of thousands of abandoned vehicles and wandering horses. An impression of awful and irretrievable disaster.

I hear that General Dame has been wounded and taken prisoner; also Colonel Legrez, Chief of the Staff, Colonel Simon of the divisional training school, Colonel Bignon of the Artillery, Captains Perrier, de Lambert, Fumey—all the stars of the Staff. The General insisted, the day before yesterday, on supervising the withdrawal of our three regiments or what remained of them, for they started out with a complement of 3000 men each, and now a few hundred only remain, and they have been in action almost every day. The General was seen with the first two; then he was wounded and captured before he reached the third. Tears come to my eyes. General Dame was a man of ability. It is a loss for us and for France. Of the nine colonels of the division, seven have been killed or wounded.

Colonel Sevestre of the 13th Algerian Rifles commands the division. The men, according to their units, are distributed over the hilly dunes. They dig shelters and then fall asleep. The Vet. and I have a night's rest on a few wisps of straw in a barn.

30 *May* 1940.   Colonel Sevestre orders a count to be taken of men and officers to be embarked: 1250. That is all that remains of our fine North African Division of 18,000 men. The rest: killed, wounded, prisoners, missing.

We manage to cook some haricot beans found in abundance in abandoned British lorries; we also found corned beef, jam, cigarettes, etc. I have lost my kit, and have only what I stand up in. One of my poilus has presented me with a handkerchief. It was the only bit of spare linen he had.

At midday Colonel Sevestre sends for me. He orders us, that is, Captain Guillaume of the 13th Algerian Rifles, who commands the regiment (180 men), and myself, to embark at Dunkirk half of the remains of the division, about 550 men. My detachment consists of the men of my company who could be collected together, about 90; anti-aircraft gunners, and anti-tank units. Immediate departure, 9 miles to go, on foot. The only possible way is along the railway track; we follow this as well as we can. At Malo-les-Bains, we begin to look for the way. As usual, no guides, no military traffic control, not even a direction arrow placed by the High Command. A customs officer gives us some vague directions. Finally, a staff officer from the port of Dunkirk, whom we chance to meet, advises

Guillaume and myself to place our men in the shelter of a large building containing drainage pumps. Guillaume goes blindly ahead to get information.

The port of Dunkirk has suffered. Not a single building is intact, many have collapsed or have been burnt out. About five o'clock in the afternoon, the first shells come over. I send my men to take cover in the open ditches round the building; these are narrow enough to restrict any damage done. Now 77, 88 and 105 mm. shells are coming over, almost continuously. We huddle together in little hollows in the walls, under the pumps and dynamos.

At last, at nine o'clock, we receive the order to embark. There are seven to eight hundred yards to cover and two foot-bridges to cross. I turn out the men in groups of ten in single file. The Boches are shelling the whole port, which is immense, so the density of fire is not very great. I have retained from the last war my sense of the direction of projectiles and send the men to earth only when a shell is definitely in our neighbourhood.

The westerly wind beats down the immense columns of grim, black smoke from the flaming oil tanks. Truly this is the suffocating breath of the last judgment. Long sheaves of bright flames shoot up from the huge burning buildings. Broken bricks and mortar, windows, paving stones dislodged by shells, strew the ground. Immense open spaces stretch farther than the eye can see with only a fragment of wall standing here and there, and the carcasses of the monster cranes in the docks despairingly hold up their great black arms towards a ghastly sky, rent unceasingly by the explosions of the whining shells.

Squadrons of planes circle above us, dropping sticks of bombs in quick succession. The men flatten out on the ground, making use of stacks of coal or trucks, or anything, for protection.

We arrive at the quay-side, where other units are already waiting. An elderly commander, looking rather tired—I think his name was Kerneis—tells us that a mistake has been made and that the boats intended for us have been used for other troops. Tramp steamers might be expected in the middle of the night or next morning. Already four of my men have been killed, others seriously wounded, whilst coming from the shed to

the beach. I don't want to take them back, so I lead them into
the dunes near the lighthouse—completely unprotected, it is
true, but the Germans are aiming at the port and fire but little in
this direction. The men scatter among the dunes in little groups,
so as to minimize the risk. They drop wearily to sleep, despite the
shells ceaselessly falling a few hundred yards away. The Vet.,
wonderfully calm as usual, takes command, while I go with
Guillaume to see the Commander (who is rather limp by now)
in the casemates at the foot of the lighthouse. About 1 a.m.
Admiral 'North' (Abrial) telephones that four cargo vessels are
at the entrance to the port. Kerneis sends a sailor in a motor-
boat to tell them to come alongside. The sailor returns an hour
later, without being able to find the boats. Kerneis then tells me
that he will wait for the dawn. I make such a fuss that he sends
his man again; he returns in half an hour and says that he has
seen nothing. Fresh altercation with Kerneis, whose one desire
is to sleep. Eighty sailors are sleeping there in the casemate.
'My men are tired,' he tells me, 'and they must rest.' 'And what
about mine, who have travelled two hundred miles under atrocious conditions?' In the end he gives way and sends another
motor launch, which comes back in twenty minutes, having
found the ships.

31 *May* 1940. I arouse the men. At three o'clock in the
morning we begin to embark on two little cargo boats at the
quay-side, the *Keremah* and the *Hebe*; I board the latter. In
the dim light of the dawn, we can see the British embarking
from a wooden wharf, on the other side of the dock, for we
each have our own quay-side in order to avoid confusion and
friction. Their position does not seem to be as good as ours, a
shell or a bomb would cut their wharf in two at any moment.

At four o'clock we steam out through heavy shelling. Fortunately, all the shells fall on the quay, or in the water, for
shortly afterwards the captain, a fine fellow from Quimper, tells
me that his old tub is loaded with melinite, bombs and hay which
he was to have unloaded at Dunkirk, but which he is now taking
back to Dover. British warships are at intervals along the route
to Dover, where we arrive after a crossing lasting four hours.

Arrival at Dover

As soon as we disembark we are all struck by the general orderliness and strict discipline. We march into the customs sheds where we all lay down our arms, except the officers. Fine buffet loaded with sandwiches varied to suit your taste, tea, cheese. Later we go downstairs and lead the men to the station.

I wanted to go out into the street to buy a few things, a shirt, a toothbrush, etc., since I have nothing but what I stand up in. I was refused, and for the moment, I was angry, but I admit that I was wrong. An order is an order and must be obeyed.

I was stupid enough to let my first detachment go on ahead whilst I waited for the second, under the command of Jans and the Vet., who were on the *Keremah*. I waste my time waiting until eleven in the evening. During this time I talk to a staff officer of the 1st Army. He tells me that when we prepared to attack in order to join Frère's army, two British divisions were supposed to participate in the operation. At the last minute they were withdrawn and went off to embark at Dunkirk. Why did they do that? Would the attack have succeeded? I shall probably never get to the bottom of the matter. Perhaps they did the best thing in getting back to England; if they are still intact, they will be able to land somewhere else in France.

At 11 p.m. I return to the station. Trains steam out every ten minutes. We travel until eleven o'clock next morning. At each station, crowds of young women and old gentlemen bring us sandwiches, tea, lemonade, cigarettes, cakes, postcards to write home; all with the utmost kindness. I express the wish to send a telegram to my sister. An elderly gentleman undertakes to do it and refuses the money that I offer for the telegram. These people cannot do enough by way of being kind. They receive us as brothers rather than allies.

1 *June* 1940.   At Plymouth, a house, with dining-room, rest rooms, bath-rooms, is especially set aside for French officers. I am in great pain with my right foot which is very swollen; it appears to be an attack of arthritis brought on by fatigue and bad food during the last twenty days. Set out for the docks at one o'clock, limping worse than ever. An English officer takes

me in his car to the *El Dezaire*, an auxiliary cruiser, Pacquet Co. steamer, requisitioned for the transport of troops.

I am first on board. The ship's doctor takes me to the sick bay and diagnoses an acute swelling due to my attack of arthritis. A male nurse, a monk in private life, washes my feet (I'm sorry for him); I am given a cabin and sleep until seven in the evening. The steamer has not weighed anchor.

Dinner (three services for 125 surviving officers on board). At 8.30 p.m. I go back to bed. The steamer gets under way at about 10 o'clock. At 4 a.m. we are just off Cherbourg, where we land at 4 o'clock in the afternoon. My foot and ankle are tremendously swollen. I ask to be driven to the train which will take my men to Bernay where the North African divisions are to be regrouped. My request is refused and I am taken to the large naval hospital and placed in a common room for officers, all the private rooms being occupied. During these two days spent with a number of officers from other divisions of the army in Flanders, I hear innumerable facts which bear out the vastness of the disaster. All divisions have suffered as much as ours. The total strength saved is paltry. Several Generals have been captured with their staffs. I learn that our excellent friend Général Billotte has died under what we were purposely led to believe were mysterious circumstances. He was in command of the Northern armies and Weygand, we were told, would have wanted to held him partly responsible for the disaster—Weygand came by plane about ten days ago to give orders. Allusions were made to what was called a violent scene between Weygand, Blanchard, Prioux and Billotte. After Weygand had left, Billotte had a fatal car accident—overtaking a lorry his driver collided with another car coming from the opposite direction. The ridiculous rumour was spread that he had committed suicide. I do not believe a word of it, this great leader would never have done such a thing. What a tragedy for his charming wife! My sister also will be very grieved.

On sailing out of Dunkirk, I had seen a boat sink as a result of striking a parachute mine dropped, so I was told, by an enemy plane.

The same morning, after leaving St Malo or Bray-Dunes, the

Loss of the Sirocco

Sirocco, that glorious destroyer, was sunk out at sea by a Boche motor torpedo boat which sneaked through the Anglo-French defences. We had several survivors on board. It is estimated that about 300 men were drowned; no life-belts had been given out, there were not enough to go round. All those who could swim or had belts were quickly saved by the British boats in the neighbourhood.

Another destroyer received a bomb on the stern, just as she set sail; it was possible to tow her, with her load of troops, to Dover.

All officers complain bitterly of the failure of the High Command after the first days of the battle to organize any traffic control. We are certain that with a little organization the heavy units of the army could have been freed much more quickly and so have embarked, with the aid of the great cranes of Dunkirk, which remained undamaged, precious war supplies, such as guns, tanks, anti-tank guns, anti-aircraft guns which would thus have been saved instead of being left in the hands of the enemy; they would have been damaged, of course, but not beyond repair.

A tremendous loss of money to be sure, but also an irreparable loss of enormous quantities of material which we shall miss sorely in the next Boche offensive in which his army, released from Flanders, will be able to open out a gigantic offensive on the southern front. All those who fought in 1914–1918 say that the High Command not only has not improved on the organization existing then, but has almost forgotten it. An impression that I have had a hundred times. Its heart-rending!

All the officers of the light-armoured divisions and the anti-tank units criticize the use made of them in placing them in small groups, useless for large-scale front line operations or in employing them for ridiculous jobs, such as guarding cross-roads. One feels that all are terribly uneasy on the issue of the war, after having been buoyed up with hope, just before entering Belgium. The poilus joined together in roundly cursing the total lack of aeroplanes; that strikes them most. The officers agree.

Of two naval officers, one maintains that Germany entered the war with 15,000 planes, the other that they had 20,000. During the last few months, 3000 have been destroyed, but how many have they been able to make during the last nine months? And we announce in enormous headlines in the newspapers that 1500 have been ordered from the United States!

As for the tanks brought into operation in recent battles by the Germans, all the officers of the light-armoured divisions are amazed at their numbers. They have constantly had to struggle one against four, sometimes one against ten.

English newspapers are pessimistic about Italy. Her entry into the war is expected in less than a week. What will happen to our communications with Syria? Italy is credited with the intention of first seizing the Balkans and then attacking Egypt.

Another destroyer *La Bourrasque* has been sunk in the open sea by a magnetic mine, between Dunkirk and Dover. As it was broad daylight, only 150 men were drowned.

The food in the Naval Officers' Hospital is abundant and good. We exchange ideas and impressions. Many officers place the responsibility for our disaster not only on the High Command, but also on our politicians. This opinion, they say, is unanimously held by all, our indignation comes from the heart, we are full of hatred against France's murderers. And who are they? The Government composed of disreputable and hated people is still in office, at a time when new blood—military men with a grip on things—is needed. It is an insult to the Motherland, to the Army, to all those who have given their lives to their country and to us, who are ready to do so. This stupid régime will lead us to defeat and to ruin, if we do not hurl it quickly into the gutter. Those are the utterances I often hear.

2 *June* 1940.   Alert about one o'clock in the morning. Some planes drop a few bombs.

3 *June* 1940.   Alert about 2.30 a.m. The firing of the anti-aircraft guns can be heard plainly; the planes are mine-layers on their way out over the sea. They drop mines to which parachutes are attached, generally magnetic mines. To-morrow, trawlers will sweep the channel; working in pairs—they themselves being

demagnetized by electrified cables passing under the hull—with electromagnets attached to the sweeping cables to explode the mines as the sweep approaches them. The British sweep in this way too, also with magnetic sweeps between low flying planes skimming the water.

A sub-lieutenant tells us that at Calais they were warned long before 10 May to be very suspicious of Belgian trawlers seen moving up and down those waters, as they were suspected of laying mines and sweeping up those laid by the French.

Spying in Belgium and in the North of France has been terrifyingly rampant; everyone has noticed that hardly had a battery been moved up into position, or a wood, copse or farm been occupied than half-an-hour later German guns would open fire or their air force would start bombing. At Dunkirk we saw suspicious lights coming from little huts in the direction of the outgoing fairway. As soon as our vessels entered the channel, the secret lights would operate and the artillery would redouble its intensity in the exact direction of the ships.

Dispenser Charbonnier, at our hospital, had five persons shot, one a beautiful young girl; by showing lights and curtains of different colours, they had guided German aircraft, signalling to them and thereby causing fires in the neighbouring chemical factory. Elsewhere, two individuals had barricaded themselves behind the trap-door of a loft and had to be shot through the skylight in the roof. Everywhere were to be seen a considerable number of down-and-out creatures, without any papers, unshaven, tatterdemalions feigning idiocy. The order was given throughout the whole of Belgium to remove the glazed advertisement panels of a certain brand of chicory, PACHA CHICORY, behind which, thanks to a special chemical re-agent, information useful to the enemy was revealed.

4 *June* 1940. Cherbourg rather heavily bombed at midnight by planes which, coming from inland, caught the anti-aircraft units napping. Our warning came from the peculiar whistling of machines dive-bombing. Twelve to fifteen bombs of heavy calibre fell on the port and arsenal.

A fresh alert towards two o'clock; mine-layers are at work;

one single explosion, a mine must have fallen on the ground or exploded on coming into contact with the water, its parachute having failed to open.

Sub-lieutenant Philippe, a charming lad, was at Dunkirk. He explains to us how, by means of ultra-waves (sound waves emitted from the earth, I believe, and which, reflected from the aeroplanes, return to earth) one can follow continuously the progress of German raiding machines, their departure from the aerodrome, their course, number and altitude. The apparatus used is English. He was giving this information to our anti-aircraft units and our air force, but the latter, being short of machines, could do nothing. In the north, there existed three or four of these posts, at Lille, Calais and Dunkirk. All have fallen into enemy hands, destroyed for certain; these equipments are rare and we miss them badly now. If we had numerous, powerful fighter aircraft, there would be a good chance of intercepting the raiders or fighting them effectively.

On several airfields, planes had been set on fire, always in the same place, round about the tail, by small delayed-action incendiary bombs placed there by parachutists or by fifth column swine. This is shocking but true enough, since Dispenser Charbonnier, Doctor Chabaud and a naval lieutenant have actually seen a number of machines burned out in this way.

I learn that two French divisions in the frontier zone, reinforced by tanks and artillery from other divisions in retreat, undertook the defence of Dunkirk under the command of General Fagal. They fought their way inch by inch for 20 miles until they reached the outskirts of the town, burning supplies, destroying tanks and guns. The last British embarked on 1 June; leaving about 60,000 French, who were almost all able to get away from the town. The Germans captured hardly any troops at Dunkirk beyond the seriously wounded from the hospitals of Zuydcoote and Bray-Dunes.

A flying officer says that Rotterdam was taken by German parachutists. I could hardly believe it and yet it is true. This is how it is done. The parachutist must be dropped from a height of 500 to 1000 feet; for if he is released too high, he is inevitably killed by machine-gun fire from the ground, during his slow descent. On landing, the parachutist is sometimes dragged one or two hundred yards, if there is any wind, before he has time to unhook his parachute in order to free himself. He must get on his feet, readjust his equipment and join up with the other parachutists for an important operation. Even when wave after wave of planes come over, the parachutists are forced to land in dispersed order. Open country, without trees, hedges and bushes is necessary for their safe landing and subsequent assembling.

To crown all, I learn that the Germans have landed light tanks, suspended from planes fitted with extremely large wheels which are retracted during flight. On landing, the tanks are released.

All these operations were made possible by a force of the fifth column which had already taken possession of a large airfield near Rotterdam; there were no fighter planes or anti-aircraft guns in the vicinity. The fifth columnists helped the parachutists to their feet, grouped them together and directed them towards the key-positions of the city, the station, the central telephone exchange, the barracks, the gas-works, etc. But at the Hague, where a few troops showed their determination by shooting the parachutists, the result was disastrous; all were killed or made prisoners and enemy tanks could not be landed. One may conclude that a few isolated parachutists could always land, especially at night, and blow up a bridge or a factory. But for an attack in force to succeed, the help of a fifth column is indispensable, first to put out of action the fighters and the anti-aircraft units, then to help the landing and the assembling of the parachutists.

5 *June* 1940. Another air attack last night. The senior doctor of the hospital, who showed clear signs of an attack of nerves in the shelter during the night, has decided to evacuate the entire hospital, and to put all the sick and wounded on a hospital train. I pay a visit to the doctor treating me, Dr Watteau, who promises to keep me; I feel much better and ask to be sent back to my division as soon as possible. But at three o'clock in the afternoon I am told that I must go too. Once more I visit the

senior doctor; he refuses to keep me, having decided to evacuate the whole hospital. His nerves appear to me to be extremely bad, and he asks me not to insist. Perhaps he has got information concerning the situation?

6 *June* 1940.   Departure at five o'clock. We are very comfortably placed on stretchers in three tiers, fifteen officers in a carriage for thirty. Staff very attentive; food excellent. A few wounded men are left at Vannes, then the others at Auray. After spending twenty-four hours in the train, motor coaches take us 4 miles to St Anne-D'Auray, Hôpital du Juvenat, a religious institution for girls, quite new, very modern, showers, bathrooms, etc. We are the first sick and wounded to enter, but nothing seems to be in proper order. There is repose, tranquillity and fresh air, but the food is mediocre; things do not run smoothly; these gentlemen have had only a few months in which to do nothing, and nothing is ready. Always in France we muddle through at the last moment.

I recollect that the charming sub-lieutenant, Philippe, who was at Dunkirk, had told us that at bastion No. 32, the control room of Admiral 'North' (Abrial), an order of the day was posted up stating that they were to hold on to the end. Immediately the twenty-five officers received twenty-five revolvers and thirty cartridges; the sailors had neither arms nor ammunition. The officers re-read the order of the day and gazed, thunderstruck, at their pitiful twenty-five revolvers.

I hear a few criticisms, which I believe to be unjustified, of Dautry, Minister of Munitions, whom some call 'the 6th column'. It is said that we are short of 6 to 700,000 men, who were withdrawn from the front-line and put into reserved occupations in factories, some of which, it appears, cannot be brought into production under a year. These criticisms are based on the fact that in the month of April, one month before the German offensive, we received instructions to send back, without verification, any man who signed a declaration that he was a skilled hand drawn from an amazing list, a page long. A week after a man had signed his declaration, we were compelled to send him home. If the man had made a false declaration, he was liable to prosecution and imprisonment. But if a complacent employer protected the offender, it would be extremely difficult to detect the fraud. One of my men signed the declaration so I was obliged to send him home; he was a comptometer repairer but after all he may have been an excellent mechanic!

10 *June* 1940. (*Sunday.*) A few friends and myself spend the afternoon in Auray, where the church and lower town fill us with delight. Here, as elsewhere, there are many refugees. The five o'clock newspapers are depressing: the communiqué is bad. The Germans appear to have set foot in Rouen and to the south of the Aisne. These lightning advances to the north-west and the south-east already threaten Paris. The Seine is one of the vital arteries for the provisioning of Paris in heavy goods, and this artery is cut. The attitude of Italy is more and more threatening. We return to our quarters in moody silence. Spirits rise somewhat after a good dinner, well washed down by the wines of the Hotel de France de St Anne.

11 *June* 1940. The die is cast. The radio tells us that Italy has come into the war. France is tottering, Italy takes advantage of it to stab her in the back. I had foreseen this event since the beginning of the war, nevertheless it momentarily depresses a few of my friends. After a few hours, they recover and begin to calculate their chances of being sent to the front as soon as possible. Nearly all of us do so. The communiqué is agonizing; the Germans have succeeded in crossing the Seine and are probably at Pont de l'Arche. Incredible!

The senior doctor, in answer to my request, promises to let me go to-morrow morning to Bernay where my division is being re-formed. I lie down the whole afternoon so that my foot may be fit to stand the fatigue of the journey.

No news of my sister. Has she decided at last to leave Paris? I hope so.

12 *June* 1940. I receive a letter from my sister, who has made up her mind to leave Paris and go to a sister-in-law in a little village in the Cher, some 12 miles from Bourges; perhaps

our niece Denise and her two children, one aged four months, will also be going. They are going by car. So they are to share the fate of hundreds of thousands of refugees who, for the last month, have been toiling along the roads of Belgium and France, driven like bewildered sheep before the savage hordes. At least, she is in a car; how many wretched women have I seen, in old worn-out shoes, carrying a child, swathed up, at the breast and dragging one or two tired youngsters, crying and clutching at their mother's skirt! And old couples of 75, pushing a wheelbarrow, loaded with a case and a few old clothes, falling panic-stricken, or overcome by fatigue on the bank at the side of the road. Is it possible that such crimes should find their reward in victory? I refuse to believe it.

I miss my train at 8.55 a.m. at Auray, the car lent me by the hospital having run out of petrol on the way. I take a goods train at 2 p.m. and arrive at Le Mans at 6 o'clock the next morning.

13 *June* 1940. After four hours' walking about and making inquiries among the military authorities, I learn that the divisional artillery park (my division) is 12 miles from Le Mans at St Corneille. A decent civilian, for whom I obtain four gallons of petrol from the Headquarters of the Fourth Zone, drives me there together with one of my poilus, miraculously found on the platform at Laval in the midst of a dense crowd. Major Didier and all the officers give me a rousing reception. Alas! I learn that four of their officers were left behind, killed, wounded, or prisoners in Belgium; among them is Captain Pierron, who, wounded in the chest by one or two bullets from tanks coming unexpectedly upon the column, refused to allow his men to carry him away, telling them: 'Don't bother about me, my life is finished, you have children. Embrace me and run for your lives.' This modest hero owned a small café in Paris. I was touched by the story, for Pierron was a splendid and delightful comrade.

I mess with them until I am able to rejoin the divisional staff whose exact whereabouts they do not know. All events are, of course, discussed; once more, the admirable morale of the troops is confirmed. The High Command made such bad use of it, believing perhaps that Hitler would not attack us this year. The sappers were more often employed for the construction of soldiers' clubs than for the building of blockhouses. Being men of common sense they asked themselves why they were used for those jobs of minor importance instead of equipping the frontier line. Major Didier often remained, during the Flanders campaign, without orders and out of contact with the Staff, exactly as I did. Like me, he had a gift for being able to find his way, and this enabled him to steer a course between the lines and bring his men to safety without too many losses. Events happened so quickly that our leaders were always overwhelmed; they never dared take the decision to send to the rear the heavy material and to make room to manœuvre by a retirement on a wide front. Such a movement would have been facilitated by the elimination of the heavy units and the decision not to allow the civilian exodus. I have always been of the opinion that one could, in this way, have embarked a great part of the vast quantities of supplies left in enemy hands, supplies which we sadly miss.

Captain Briand of the Engineers, whom I met on the goods train, was attached to the Staff of General Blanchard and is reticent as to his qualities as a leader but repeats what I had already heard. The General is a man of petty decisions, too quickly tired by the extremely hard work of leading even his own army, not to mention the leading of a group of armies under the same conditions. I have always been unfavourably impressed because of the intense boosting that Blanchard himself has had put abroad, or allowed others to do for him. A true chief has no need of that, especially in times so serious as these.

We listen to the wireless at 7.30 p.m., in which Paul Reynaud's message to Roosevelt is read, asking for the support, and the entry into the war, of America. We remain dumbfounded; this message is the cry of alarm and despair of the vanquished who foresee the fall of Paris; hence the Government's flight to a province of France, thence to North Africa, and then if need be, to our possessions in America. I can understand his sending this message to Roosevelt with the intention of inducing the Americans to enter the war, but to broadcast it throughout

France, to foreshadow endless withdrawals, that is defeat, the total loss of our soil. Is that the way to galvanize our troops, or to calm the fears of those behind the lines? Is it not rather the way to sow the seeds of panic? Was it necessary, or have we really reached that stage? The voting in the American Congress and Senate on the question of supplying arms and planes was pro-Ally with a large majority. Can this be a portent of the United States' entry into the war? If it is so, it will be a moral factor of the highest importance for us, and a cause for grave anxiety to the German people. I wonder if America is about to make up her mind, for President Roosevelt has authorized this message, now three days old, to be broadcast to the American people. We must wait and see. But to-day, the Germans have advanced still farther. They are less than 20 miles from Paris.

I saw, during my long journey, hundreds of British guns being towed along the roads, and at least fifty tanks being carried by rail. Is a vast counter-attack in preparation against the German units which have crossed the Seine and are now making their way down to Paris?

The wildest and most ridiculous stories are going round. It is said that Gamelin has shot four or five generals and then committed suicide when given his marching orders on being superseded by Weygand. Ridiculous! It reminds me of the idiotic tales of the last war; when Gallieni died following an operation for prostatitis, it was rumoured that he was shot in his office by General Herr.

14 *June* 1940. The disastrous news is confirmed. The Government has declared Paris an open city and troops are retreating south of the capital. Everywhere the enemy advances; one feels that the Army is incapable of any further resistance. Probably it hasn't the means to continue fighting, for that was the case in Belgium. Never were the ranks broken there, never did men shrink from any sacrifice. They were crushed beneath the weight of metal, paralysed by new tactics of which our Staff and the British had little foresight and still less knowledge. It has been said that they were ready to go to war à la 1914–18. But officers and men did their duty wherever they had the means of fighting.

Some of our friends are very much depressed. Major Didier was the first to dare say openly: 'We are done for.' Others, on the contrary, braced themselves and asked to be transferred to the Infantry where they would sell their lives dearly. But between ourselves we begin to discuss what the fate of France will be if she is beaten.

Hitler announced more than six months ago that he would be in Paris on 15 June. He will be there to the day and the hour; such exactitude is paralysing. He also declared that peace would be signed on 14 July and that he would march into Paris through the Arc de Triomphe. Did he speak the truth? I refuse to admit it. One card remains in our hands: the decision of the United States of America who would link up perhaps with other nations of South and Central America; Brazil would supply us with coffee and sugar, Columbia and Mexico with oil, Argentine with wheat, the United States with arms, aeroplanes and soldiers. Russia will perhaps realize that immediately England and ourselves are out of the struggle, her turn will come, for Hitler cannot intend his recent reconciliation to be genuine after six years of raving and ranting against Bolshevism to the Italians and his own people. But if the neutrals do not join together, how shall we resist?

The wireless announces this evening heavy troop concentrations on the German frontier. Is my forecast coming true? This very slender hope buoys us up and restores some measure of confidence to us.

I learn that the horse transport companies are being reformed at Saumur; I shall go there to-morrow, hoping to find my poilus and friends.

15 *June* 1940. I take a passing ambulance train at Le Mans, en route for Angers where I shall change for Saumur. I travel with several officers; among them is a major in the artillery who is suffering from nervous depression. He is returning from the Beauvais region where his horse-drawn 75's were in action. He fought to the end, destroying, he said, about sixty Boche tanks, but his three brigades were wiped out. (A French field artillery brigade comprised four batteries of four guns each.) The tanks

emerged quite near his guns and in such numbers that in spite of the slaughter he was able to inflict, he was submerged and forced to destroy his guns, after firing the last shell, and then abandon them. Three brigades of 75's against sixty tanks is a losing game. He thinks that we no longer have anti-tank weapons in any useful quantity. To engage horse-drawn 75's against tanks is to consign them to certain destruction.

He also complains, as the other officers do—among them some from La Bresle—that our aviation is insufficient. They have been shelled and machine-gunned and have not seen a single allied plane defending them or attacking the German lines. Everyone is sceptical as to the exploits of our machines, as announced in the communiqués; in fact I haven't met a single officer who has seen our air force at work. Has it been destroyed, or so reduced that its action is a mere fiction, like that of the anti-tank guns?

I believe that our air drama may be explained in the following manner: when two opponents are facing each other, one of them having 1000 airplanes, the other 4000, then during the first days of battle, unequal fights take place. The 1000 airplanes may perhaps perform feats of valour, even destroy 2000 enemy planes. But they are bound to be doomed by sheer weight of numbers and after a short while the 1000 planes will be reduced to nil. The enemy may have lost twice as many machines but in the end he gets air supremacy, machine-gunning and bombing at ease without meeting the slightest opposition. The army, then deprived of air protection, fights on like a blind man against a foe with a hundred eyes.

On the other hand, we are said to have had 3000 planes and that the High Command, wishing to use its reserves sparingly had, up to now, thrown only a 1000 planes into the battle. The reserve, it was said, remained far away from the front, unused, particularly in the region of Toulouse. Is this true? It seems possible. We have seen so many surprising things.

From Angers to Saumur, I travel in a Micheline carriage where we number 300, frightfully cramped together. The station superintendent tells me that the horse transport companies which were billeted some 12 miles from Saumur left yesterday and to-day for Coutras, near Bordeaux, but that motor transport companies are still there at La Verrerie, near Saumur, and will depart to-night. I hasten there, expecting to find the motor company of my division. Alas! it was a motor transport depôt which had the job of re-equipping and reorganizing motor transport headquarters. They had just refitted the 1st North African Division, and not the 2nd, which is mine. The Colonel very kindly proposed that I should leave with him on the morrow, as the depôt is moving off to Bellac. I gladly accept, for it is on the way to Bordeaux, and perhaps I shall find means of rejoining my division.

The organization of this 'C.O.R.A.' (Centre for the organization and repartition of automobiles) leaves a bad impression. Everybody quite unnecessarily remains on duty at night and the personnel is tired. The Colonel is a nice man, but lacking in energy. No command. The men in the workshop do their best, toiling through part of the night to repair requisitioned vehicles. But there is no stock of spare parts for all these cars of too many different makes. The General Staff of the 4th region asks urgently for a small van and touring-car to be used by a unit stationed at Tours which has to go to the front. After two hours' discussion no agreement had been reached concerning these two vehicles. Some officers wanted to keep the good material for themselves and send two old crocks. Others were of a different opinion. Finally they compromised. A lorry in good condition was sent accompanied by a Citroen with run-down batteries.

The cars had to be in Tours at midnight. It is 12.30. Tours, warned by telephone, agrees to wait for the cars until dawn. The Lieutenant is so tired that I offer to take his place, if he will go and lie down. Although there are fifteen officers in the 'C.O.R.A.', all are exhausted.

At 4 o'clock the two cars started for Tours. Of course at 5 o'clock the lorry returned to say that the Citroen had broken down. I am obliged to show my teeth to make a sleepy captain send his own car in its place.

Last night a wireless communiqué stated that Russia has invaded Lithuania. Why? Is it a scramble for the spoils in which everyone intends to join? Or do the Russians wish to threaten and invade Eastern Prussia?

The wireless tells us that a Cabinet meeting has been in session since 2 o'clock; it is now half-past eight and the Cabinet is still sitting and discussing, according to the first-hand statement of several officers, the surrender of France and Peace.

The swiftness of defeat is so crushing that certain officers seem unsurprised. We were so accustomed to the idea of a continuous front-line, like that of the last war, that it seems difficult to conceive how to organize resistance without it. It is impossible to rebuild a new and impregnable front, one says; what can we do under the circumstances? A moral shock is necessary to restore confidence to these good people. Everybody thinks of the U.S.A. But immediately the distress reappears: when will the men, the material, the planes arrive? How can we keep on until then? Has Weygand got a sufficient man-power— French and English—to counter-attack and stop the Boches? There is evidence that something is in preparation in Western France. This idea is sufficient to inspire new hope in everyone.

No news of my sister. Did she arrive at Aix d'Anguillon near Bourges? Will she remain there, with the Germans continually advancing?

17 *June* 1940.   Yesterday we reached Bellac (Haute-Vienne) by car, in company with a dignified white-bearded officer, Major Marechal. Like me, he has the fighting spirit, the spirit of the last war, he is alert and game for anything. All day long for ten hours we have freed traffic jams at cross-roads and have tried to set in orderly motion the great flood of refugee cars. When night came our voices were hoarse, our legs shaky, our shirts wet through, but we felt that we had done some good.

This morning's communiqué is most depressing; the Germans are in Burgundy, at Dijon and Auxerre and are now pushing on to Laigle and Flers in Normandy. One feels that all is lost and that the Army can no longer resist anywhere.

The Colonel commanding the depôt sent for me. Captain Poncet and myself are to go in search of 1100 ambulances, lorries and vans abandoned probably in the neighbourhood of

Orleans—Pithiviers, Olivet, and Cercotte. If we find these vehicles, we are to phone to Bellac, whence a sufficient number of drivers will be despatched. The order was countermanded just as we were starting; the Germans will be there before us.

18 *June* 1940. We learn by wireless that Pétain and Weygand have asked for an armistice. Several officers weep bitterly. Others remain indifferent as if struck dumb by the disaster; we all discuss the news, which has not surprised us, for last night's wireless gave us to understand that Pétain would have to make a vital decision. Everyone tries to imagine what terms the enemy will impose; most of us are very pessimistic and expect atrocious conditions.

My mind is made up; I shall try to get to England and join up as a volunteer. Hardly had I said this when ten, fifteen, twenty of my friends decided to throw in their lot with me. I cannot believe that France, which has taken a thousand years to develop and has acquired a splendid colonial empire, will die within a month at the hands of a butcher. During a great part of the night I ponder over my plan of escape, by an English ship from Bordeaux or from Le Boucaut, or through Spain or Portugal.

19 *June* 1940. Hasty departure from Bellac; it appears that the Boches are not far away. The Colonel has entrusted me with the formation of a large company for the headquarters of a light motorized division. Hope revives. I am acting in company with Captain Quille, who will command the Service Corps of the motorized forces. I have eleven officers and six hundred men, but only thirty-five ambulances and five Withe lorries—a mere nothing.

Departure at 9.30 p.m. for Mussidan, where we shall receive fresh orders. We arrive at 5 a.m. after a lovely night's travelling through hilly and wooded country. Some of the natives of Mussidan and some refugees from Rouen—charming young women and girls—welcome us in their delightful houses and there we stay until two o'clock in the afternoon. These people tell us that on the previous evening a young general, General de

Gaulle, a former military adviser to Paul Reynaud, declared on the London radio that he was enrolling a French army in England where he would receive all officers and men and civilian workers from the engineering industries. The superiority in equipment of the British would soon show itself, he said. France is, for the moment, beaten, but we shall smash the Boches on other battlefields. The *Journal* has published an article announcing that the British are making 60-ton tanks, veritable travelling fortresses in which fifteen men, behind armour plating, elastically mounted, can remain for 10 to 12 days. De Gaulle seems to be very convincing, very inspiring. Our hearts are filled with hope; our minds are made up; we are going to write to de Gaulle to enlist and to fight elsewhere. It is announced that Winston Churchill has declared that henceforth British and French will have dual nationality. De Gaulle would not have been allowed to use the microphone if he had not had the full accord of the British Government. We arrive at Saint Denis de Pile, to the south of Coutras, in the evening.

20 *June* 1940. We link up with No. 4 Motor Depôt at Coutras. They are very disappointed when we arrive with a pitiful thirty-five ambulances, instead of the hundred and fifty to two hundred that we should have had.

I am billeted in a very tiny room in a large chateau, and there, in the evening, I hear the French radio repudiate de Gaulle, whom his chiefs recall to France. What a rude awakening! We still entertain a hope that this is merely on principle while the armistice conditions are under discussion. Meanwhile the news fills us with gloom. But we are determined, whatever the cost, to make for England, Morocco, Spain, anywhere rather than remain with the Boches.

21 *June* 1940. Departure at 3 a.m. from Saint Denis de Pile with priority order to cross the Dordogne. It is incredible, despite Pétain's communiqué of last night in which he attempted to explain that our armies, cut off from each other, with enormous gaps between them, were still continuing the fight, but without hope. We are under the impression that Pétain pre-

vents his army from fighting; that he only thinks of his
Armistice. Cherbourg is taken. How could a great military
town, with forts and war-vessels lying in harbour, be taken
without a fight? It bowls one over!

Halt at Sauveterre-de-Guyenne, where we spend the night.
No. 4 Motor Depôt appears on the scene and pushes us forward
like a herd of cattle; all the men are trooping in masses, along
road after road towards the south—especially the heavy aviation equipment—and a few more or less isolated infantry
regiments, but all are without arms! Why not tell us where
to go as they did at Dunkirk? Are we a herd blindly fleeing
the ogre, or has the General Staff a comprehensive evacuation
scheme such as was carried out at Dunkirk? Alas! I don't
think so and we all have the same impression. Yet, there is a
rumour to the effect that our air force has gone to Oran and
thirty boats a day are engaged in taking troops from Bordeaux.
Where to? Morocco, or England? Is it really true?

Now people are trying to get used to the idea of seeing the
Boches arrive, since Pétain has told them there was no longer
any hope. Communiqués lose their interest; there have been
no newspapers for three days; crushed by disaster, everyone
lives just for the present trying to get something to eat in the
early morning and to buy some food for the evening. The poor
people of these parts try to persuade themselves that their lot
may be less terrible than they thought at first; they will remain
French, the Boches occupying the north and east of France.
In order to break moral resistance the fifth column spreads
reports that the Germans do not maltreat civilians, if they
come, they say, you will receive them. In 1870 they came and
went away again. You must obey the orders of the Marshal.

The behaviour of civilians towards officers has already under-
gone a noticeable change. During the last few days they have
been treated with a marked lack of respect. The people, embittered by defeat, do not distinguish between those officers
who, on the whole, have fought admirably, sustaining grievous
losses, and the High Command, which as I see it, has not been
able to fulfil its task. Never have Frenchmen seen their country
accept defeat after a month of battle: they do not understand

and place the responsibility on the Command as a whole. If Great Britain should lose the war, if we should be unable to avenge our defeat, not only will it not be an asset to have been in command, but a liability 'vae victis'.

Along the roads, at the entrance to the farms, we meet weird people in the most unexpected garb standing at little picket posts; these are civilians, good people who would like to be useful, to do something. Some are in straw hats, others in soldiers' helmets picked up from the road-side and armed with sporting-guns. They stop cars, and with hurried or tragic gestures, pretend to check one's orders. Usually they have erected an anti-tank barrier consisting of an old cart and a couple of logs balanced on four stones. All this, as well as the obstacles made by the military themselves, seems childish in comparison with the formidable weapons, the discipline and method employed by the Germans. Since the days when I arrived on the Maginot Line and in front of the northern fortifications, I have always been surprised at the niggardliness of our defences. I expressed myself cautiously on examining the earth-works, and in particular the anti-tank ditches, being of the opinion that these barriers were not **unsurmountable obstacles to the armoured divisions. My friend Desouches, I remember, was quite indignant** because of my touch of scepticism; and, not wishing to appear a defeatist or to undermine his confidence, I made a pretence of retracting my opinion and agreeing with him. And yet...how great was the dismay of Vandenbusche and myself when on returning to France from Belgium, to the north of Saint Amand, we found that the Germans had broken through our defence lines in no time. But, it is said, anything may happen; were the pill-boxes unoccupied in this sector when the Hun broke through? Those of Valenciennes most certainly were. In the end, one doesn't know what to believe. People had got so much into the habit of saying at every step that Hitler would not attack this year, and perhaps never, that in the end nothing was done to equip the pill-boxes.

During the three or four months preceding the German attack in May, the papers which submerged us in ever-growing quantity dealt only with soldiers' clubs, the organization of amusements and army theatres. Our divisional staff talked at length of the next performance at the theatre at Anzin in which Josephine Baker would appear; I myself, catching the prevailing tone, organized Saturday evening dances at Maing where I had got together the makings of a jazz band. The sappers were taken from their work of constructing pill-boxes and put on to huts for soldiers' clubs, stages for shows, scenery, etc.

In short, our High Command had learned nothing, understood nothing, and had no information about the preparations, the capacity and the tactics of the enemy, despite the campaigns in Poland and Norway. To be sure, the enemy had used motorized columns at great speed against the opposing force and behind the lines; but we could afford to smile; the Germans had only the Poles and Norwegians to deal with, and no Maginot Line. Ah! the nations would see when we stood up to them. Alas! the nations have seen.... Now, after a lapse of a few weeks, trying to form a general picture of what has happened, I can see that we had an army, whose morale and courage were equal to that of the last war's army; save a restricted number of persons misled by hostile propaganda, everybody, workers and soldiers alike, animated by the traditional courage of Frenchmen, did his best. Two important breakdowns occurred: that of the political leadership and of the High Command. To be sure, we had not enough tanks and planes; but according to all I have heard and seen, the High Command has used our armoured forces in an absurd manner, dispersing them in small units—three here, five others there—to guard the roads; the Boches arrived in great strength, crushing one small unit after the other, whereas tanks must be employed 'en masse', to break through the enemy lines to surround the infantry, to cut adverse formations into several pieces; the tank is the modern cavalry; it is therefore necessary to use cavalry tactics: nobody would think of dispersing his cavalry into small units in order to achieve victory; it is necessary to keep great masses charging the enemy, swooping down on his rear, disorganizing his supply lines and so on. The tank, like the cavalry, is an offensive weapon; only under exceptional conditions should it be used in defence; and when used for defence purposes, it must still be employed in great quantity to counter-attack and by this means to delay the enemy's advance.

Those niggardly tactics of using tanks in small units prove a lack of comprehension concerning the use of armoured forces, with the result that, in Belgium, after four or five days, our best motorized divisions had lost 40 to 50 per cent of their strength. It seems that during the Somme battle certain generals showed a better understanding and organized an offensive, which, for reasons I still ignore, did not develop, perhaps through lack of sufficient means, perhaps because the right tactics were employed only by certain units. There can be no doubt that if the High Command displayed such a lack of strength on the whole front, our army has been crushed because it was dispersed into these small units; having been cut into a great number of sections, it was incapable of resistance. Our artillery certainly behaved heroically, sacrificing themselves to the last gun and destroying hundreds of German tanks; but afterwards, when the Boches no longer met any organized resistance in their advance, they could afford to neglect the isolated opposition, which they by-passed, thus continuing to advance 40–80 kilometres daily, leaving neither the time nor the room for us to regroup our forces.

And I think that perhaps we may have had arms in sufficient quantity and quality to resist and to beat the enemy and that our disaster could have been avoided, if our High Command had been equal to its task.

A certain restlessness is visible among the men, who cannot understand why they are condemned to inaction. They see thousands of military cars, singly or in convoy, going southwards; 'Why are we stuck here?' they ask. 'If the war is over, send us back to our homes; if it is to continue, clearly they want to hand us over to the Boches, since we have no arms.' It is rumoured that the enemy is very near. Captain Quille, having emerged from a state of stupor, caused by too many drinks, into something like lucidity and good sense, assembled his men and held forth to them in popular language, promising them that if they would stick to him, he would take them home in ambulances. He is cheered and in fact quietens the men down, although his promises lack foundation and are clearly ridiculous. Many of us officers refused to remain near him while he was talking to the men. These brave fellows, who followed through thick and thin in Flanders and again at Dunkirk, would have understood quite a different message, one appealing to their courage and their love of the home-land. They would have responded to nobler words, more willingly, than to promises of surrender and a return to comfort.

Our sole topic of conversation, in the mess and elsewhere, is how to get to England. No one can understand why the French Army was not embarked; if 335,000 men could be saved in such difficult and perilous conditions as those at Dunkirk, one or two million fighting men could have been embarked for Algeria and England from all the Atlantic and Mediterranean ports: Nantes, La Rochelle, Bordeaux, Pauillac, le Boucaut, St Jean-de-Luz, Port-Vendres, Marseilles, Toulon, Nice. What purpose will be served by an armistice which will deliver us up bound and starving and at our enemy's mercy, forced to work for him against our ally, with whom we made a solemn pact not to make a separate peace? Once more we shall be perjured and forced to throw ourselves on the word of Hitler; the word that he gave to Austria, to Czecho-Slovakia, to Poland has meant nothing to our politicians. Poland, Holland, Czecho-Slovakia, even Belgium had the decency not to sign, not to bend the knee; and we, who had pledged our word to Great Britain, do we deserve, because of this treachery, any better treatment? The Germans themselves will, with reason, despise us all the more. Their interest is; undoubtedly for the moment, to appear relatively mild and correct in their behaviour towards us, but if Great Britain should succumb also, our fate will be all the more terrible.

In any case we all regard Pétain and Weygand as two old men who serve as a screen for the clique of politicians who have seized power. One has always the right not to acquiesce in the murder of one's own country, and our one desire is to regain our liberty.

I decide to go in search of information at Bayonne.

De Gaulle disowned

22 *June* 1940. Departure with Lieutenant Dagommer. On the roads, enormous convoys of heavy aviation equipment are making for the south, we think, for the purpose of embarking. At the British Consulate at Bayonne we are told by the British and French Military attachés that the Consul has already departed, and that they are about to do likewise. They give us the impression of being in mad haste, as if the devil were at their heels. While rushing downstairs, where we perforce accompany them, they tell us that it is forbidden to enlist in England, and that even if we managed to reach that country, we should be considered as deserters. They add that de Gaulle has been disowned and relieved of his command by the Government. Dagommer and I are dumbfounded and feel sick at heart at the attitude of these two panic-stricken fugitives.

Upon reflection, we go to the local army offices. There a captain informs us that the embarkation of all men between the ages of 17 and 45 was forbidden that morning. Being over that age, I could go, but I have promised my fellow-officers to return, and I do not wish to break my word. The officer adds that the order has just been issued for the arrest of all unattached officers in Bayonne, to take them to a depôt and to impound their cars.

Sadly we wander about the town littered with a hundred thousand cars, among a cosmopolitan crowd of Jews, Czechs, Belgians, Spaniards, British and French. We saunter along the quay-side; a Belgian cargo-boat is taking passengers on board without much supervision and from a chat with a sailor we get the impression that for the price of a few hundred franc notes we could go aboard and get to Casablanca without much trouble. But after that? What sort of reception would Casa offer us? And what would our comrades think? We tear ourselves away and resist temptation, especially for the sake of our friends and fearing they might think we wanted to save our skins.

Dagommer has some friends, the Castaings, living in a very beautiful villa on the cliffs at Bidart; he thinks that his wife and three children may be there. We receive a very warm welcome. Monsieur Castaing tells us that all foreign soldiers, Poles, Belgians, Czechs are embarking at Bordeaux and at St Jean-de-

Luz. He places his house at our disposal should we wish to try to escape from the immense concentration camp that France is about to become. Madame Dagommer is not there.

To avoid arrest at Bayonne, we go round by Cambo and the Bridge of Urt over the Adour. We dine on the bank at the side of the road in complete peacefulness, and in a lovely setting; delicious Bayonne ham and a bottle of good white wine complete the meal. Alas! Why is it that a profound inner sadness takes possession of us, denying us, perhaps for ever, complete and unalloyed joy? We return at two o'clock in the morning, a glorious night.

23 *June* 1940. Germany has compelled us to sign the armistice with Italy, our agreement with her coming into force six hours after our signing with her ally. What a fresh disgrace! Yielding to Italy without a fight, and she not having taken a single French village! The wildest rumours circulate on the conditions imposed by Germany. In reality no one knows anything.

Captain Maillard of the 1st A.S.C. tells us that he was held a prisoner by the Germans in Rennes, when he was at the Headquarters of the 10th Area. In a moment, the square in which his lorry stood was surrounded by enemy motor machine guns and tanks. Politely the German officers make the French drivers alight, and replace them by Germans; they take the field kitchens—in which the meals were already prepared, saying: 'Not for you, for us.' But they left Captain Maillard his car, the workshop lorry and one more lorry to take away the men, to whom they said: 'You are lucky, the war is over for you, you can return home.' But they inquired if there were any British among them; they appear to have a terrible grudge against them. Captain Maillard told his men to take a southerly direction; he himself, being next door to the Headquarters of the 10th Area, went there for orders.

At the same time, a staff lieutenant is seen talking calmly to a German sergeant-major; they are walking together. The German speaks French and, addressing the whole staff and the General himself, tells them that they are prisoners. No one protests, or seeks to understand, or flee the town (which is however of considerable size) in order to reach a non-invaded zone. There they stay, at their work, putting their papers in order, very calm and resigned, as if the whole matter had been foreseen.

Captain Maillard asks for orders from his superior officer, who replies: 'What can I say to you? The General has received an order from Marshal Pétain not to oppose any resistance. Rennes has been declared an open town. We have no right to fire even a single shot. We remain here, because those are the Marshal's orders.'

Maillard goes from one officer to another, asking what he must do. Everywhere the same apathy, the same submission to events; no reaction whatsoever. He returns to the commanding officer and tells him that he intends to try to escape to the non-occupied zone. There is nothing that can be done, but here is just one recommendation: 'Don't shoot, you might make it unpleasant for yourself since those are the Marshal's orders.'

An hour and a half later, Maillard comes out, walks past the solitary German sergeant-major still on guard at the door, and beckons to his subaltern; they go to their car, left in a side street behind the staff offices. As the Germans have entered Rennes from the south, Maillard, his subaltern and his chauffeur go off to the north, skirt the town without meeting anyone, then turn south. Twice they see the German motorized columns speeding west. They drive their car alongside a hedge towards the main road, and as soon as there is a short break in the German convoy, they cross the main road at speed without any trouble.

That is how the whole General Staff of the 10th Area, including the General himself, surrendered to a German sergeant-major. If Maillard was able to get away at the end of an hour and a half, others could have followed suit by hiding themselves in the town and putting on civilian clothes. The twenty or thirty officers and the fifty secretaries ought to have been able to deal with the N.C.O. and clear out ready for any service; but to surrender like that, without offering any resistance, without stirring a finger, can you wonder at the contempt of the Germans for us and our staff officers? These orders of Pétain are incomprehensible, provided he has not got something up his sleeve, for Pétain is incapable of committing treason; this thought flashes through my mind, but I dismiss it because it cannot be true. Perhaps he wishes to organize resistance in the Empire, in Africa; but to resist we must be many; therefore troops and material must be embarked—and we are not allowed to leave? We fail to understand any more.

The startling defeat of the French Army has stunned our staff officers. These courageous men fail completely to understand how it has come about. They doubt themselves, and need a mental shock to shake them from the nightmare into which they have been plunged.

That this recovery will come I am certain, for I know that France is not dead and cannot die...but when and how?

When the rout spread to the banks of the Seine, a large part of the Army, feeling that it no longer had any power to struggle against the weight of metal thrown against it, fell into a hypnotic, dream-like state. It was so even with the regular officers, as well as with the majority of staff officers; its one desire was to take shelter behind anything that would replace the armour of the tanks which it lacked. Then it retreated behind rivers, as if rivers, even with their bridges in ruins, could have proved an obstacle to the Germans for more than an hour or two. It filled me with amazement to hear: 'We will halt them at the Aisne, at the Marne, at the Seine, or even at the Loire.' Why the Loire, when neither the Meuse, the Oise, nor the Bresle had brought them to a stand? The war was always, in their imagination, the war of 1870 or 1914. To the end three-quarters of the men and officers understood nothing, crushed as they were by this blitzkrieg and lightning defeat.

Captain Maillard had hardly gone, when one of our companions introduced to us a friend, who also was bewildered by this war which he did not understand, a lieutenant in the Army Service Corps who also claims to have been taken twice by the Germans, then released with a couple of gallons of petrol in his tank and orders to return home. So the young man is on his way to rejoin his wife, who is staying at a seaside place near Bordeaux. What a mentality! No one, other than a German officer or N.C.O., has ordered him to go home. But since it is the Germans who have told him to go, he obeys them rather than his French superiors. The German is already the master; the orders of a Boche N.C.O. command more respect than those of a French General.

And it all seems quite natural; even to Captain Quille, a good fellow, after all, hero of the last war, patriot to the core, who this morning is already drinking his fourth 'pernod'. Is he trying to drown his grief, not to think any more? He makes a present to this young officer, whom he does not know, but whose story he believes without further confirmation, of one of our cars to enable him to get home; for this worthy young man, carless but impelled by the Boche's orders to turn his back on the French Army, would have to walk 25 or 30 miles. That wouldn't be very nice for him, and still more unkind to the German gentlemen who have so generously demobilized him on the fringes of a wood. When I hear that, I am nearly suffocated with shame and indignation.

That good fellow Maillard, and later many another, tells us of the seeming politeness of the Germans in giving petrol to French officers and to refugees to enable them to continue their way, policing the towns that they have taken, disentangling the traffic-blocks, helpful to all, demobilizing men and officers. And everybody gapes with astonishment. Don't the fools understand that it isn't with vinegar that flies are caught? The Germans, after having beaten us by deeds of arms, seek to vanquish us morally and drive a wedge between us and the British. Later we shall witness a change of tone, we shall see what living conditions will be imposed on us by these polite gentry who hate the English like poison.

What astonishes the French, and with reason, is the faultless organization of the German army; every column of occupation has several French interpreters, a reserve of lorry drivers ready to drive off in the cars and trucks taken from us, police who take possession of a town and restore order and discipline.

How obviously different from the organization foreseen by our own High Command, which failed to take mobile warfare into consideration and thought only of a stationary war; probably one of the causes of our defeat. They must have brought their organization to a pitch of perfection to bring from the depth of Germany, in ever sufficient quantity, those infantry trucks with drivers and interpreters, bridge-builders and sappers ready at all moments to build bridges, and repair roads; to bring all the food, munitions and spare parts for running repairs, and the vast quantities of everything necessary to maintain and propel forward a formidable army such as theirs. I picture our army in similar conditions. Our unhappy advance of some 90 miles into Belgium cost us roads jammed with traffic, orders arriving four or five hours late, food, munitions arriving sometimes, or not at all. We had to make shift all along the way. The liaison officers sought for days those for whom their messages were intended; their instructions were insufficient, they were short of motor-cycles and cars. We had no interpreters, no reserves of food, no convoys following us up closely to replace food and munitions consumed. Dozens of times we were told that the quartermaster had nothing to dole out to us, and that we must do the best we could and live on the country. Then hours would be wasted in killing a cow, finding bread or potatoes. It must have been very different with the Germans; otherwise they would not have been able to do what they did. The Government adopted a cheese-paring policy of refusing motor-cycles, liaison cars and trucks to its finest shock troops so as not to waste petrol, and to avoid being forced to requisition a few civilian cars for fear of displeasing and disturbing the elector of to-morrow. That is what is at the bottom of those emasculated pygmies' thoughts, those politicians and those politician-generals who have brought us to our present plight. And yet, as in 1914–18, they could have done anything with the soldier, that admirable French soldier who responds to every demand made on him.

Other officers pass through Sauveterre de Guyenne, telling us that the Germans, when they have the means, are taking French officers prisoner. To be on the safe side, several of my friends and myself go and buy a few civilian clothes; pull-over, a beret and blue duck trousers. We were well advised, for at two o'clock in the afternoon our orderly N.C.O. at the police-station brought us an official message informing us that the Germans were only 6 miles away, and that they would pass through Sauveterre very shortly, and we were ordered not to fire at them.

Captain Quille drives off to the Motor Depôt H.Q. at Pellegrue to get orders.

I have 74,000 francs in banknotes and 25,000 francs in Treasury bills. I assemble the officers and divide the 74,000 francs between them, on trust; then I burn the 25,000 francs worth of bills in the presence of two of them who sign my official report.

We then wait calmly, but ready to slip on our civilian clothes in order to escape into the non-occupied zone; the men are confined to their quarters and the town appears empty of troops.

At 4 p.m., Quille returns with the order to fall back 4 or 5 miles to the south, to Rimons d'Albret, off the main roads and in a wooded region where we shall be able to hide men and vehicles. Departure at 5 p.m. The Germans have not appeared. We are easily able to camouflage our detachment in the tiny village of Rimons which is lost among the well-wooded hills.

24 *June* 1940. A day of waiting. We send despatch riders to Sauveterre. The Germans have made no appearance there. Were those telephone calls the work of the fifth column?

The wireless announces that the armistice with Italy has been signed. Hostilities will cease at nightfall. Italy, we are told, has demanded, on signing the peace, the handing over of Tunisia, Corsica, Nice, Savoy and Dauphiné. Is it possible that our General Staff can have agreed to such conditions? What is the use of such an armistice if we are to be dismembered from the start? It is true that our enemies have no need to arrange anything in advance; since we are disarmed, without a fleet, without colonies from whom we might have received aid, they will be able to take just what they like. How can we stop them? I take Captain Quille aside and tell him my intention of leaving the next morning in an attempt to embark for England or Portugal. He approves and says that his sympathies are with me; he offers me his big Renault, which I must return to him with the chauffeur.

Lack of a passport

But I learn a little later that the big Renault has mysteriously disappeared, stolen, it is said; Quille and his adjutant, Lieutenant Beretti, a venomous little devil of the regular army who never showed any desire to fight, cannot explain this singular and suspicious disappearance. Quille also tells me that the only decent car remaining is a front wheel drive Citroen, and that has some damage done to it which has put it out of action. I understand and I say nothing.

25 *June* 1940. I get up at 5.30 and turn out an ambulance driver. After filling up the tank, we drive off without his knowing where we are going. I turn towards Bayonne after leaving a letter for Quille to be handed to him at nine o'clock when I shall be far away. In this letter I tell him that in view of the peculiar disappearances and accidents to cars, I have taken an ambulance which I will return as soon as I am in the neighbourhood of Bordeaux; for knowing his attitude, I judge it best to misinform him as to the direction taken.

On the road, there are hardly any refugees now; just a few heavy lorries laden with aircraft supplies, a few soldiers singly or in small groups, unarmed, treking southwards—the same disorder to the end.

At Mont-de-Marsan, all roads leading to Dax and Bayonne are barred by gendarmes. They say that the Germans have that night taken possession of the coast and it is impossible to pass. The Spanish frontier, according to them, is also strongly guarded by customs officers, and Spanish soldiers are immediately interning Frenchmen without passports. I haven't a passport. What is to be done? I hesitate for a long time. How could I get around in Spain, knowing very little of the language and having no money? For French money can have no value on the other side of the Pyrenees.

I go back in gloomy mood, hoping to find later some other means of reaching England or one of her colonies. And I will. . . .

I return at 3 o'clock in the afternoon; Quille receives me rather coldly and with a certain embarrassment. My friends surround me, eagerly questioning, and are very down-hearted when they hear that the way to freedom is blocked at every turn.

The men's supplies are difficult to come by; they can have meat once a day only and a half ration of bread. I explain the situation to them. They are decent fellows and they understand.

Hitler announced long ago that France would sign the armistice on 25 June. That man is an evil spirit.

Stuttgart has announced the conquest of Great Britain by 31 July. We shall see!

26 June 1940.   De Gaulle has not complied with the orders and threats of the felon government of France. He continues to build up, with the whole-hearted support of London, his French Expeditionary Force; every evening at 10 o'clock, we religiously listen to his energetic and engaging words. He does not insult our Government, but he has taken his stand; he considers it as being entirely under the domination of the enemy, and appeals to all Frenchmen who are not under German pressure. A dignified and proper attitude.

Why did the military attaché at Bayonne lie to us when he told us that we should be considered as deserters on arrival in England? On the contrary, we should have immediately enlisted in de Gaulle's army. If my friends and I had returned to Bayonne the next day, I am convinced that we should have found a boat to take us to any country. It maddens me to think about it. But what is the use? It is toward the future that we must look.

I have asked the officers to return the money that I handed to them on trust, and Quille also having some funds, we have been able to pay men, N.C.O.s and officers their arrears of pay.

We can go farther afield and get better food for our men, who now begin to harass us with questions regarding demobilization. Their confidence in the illusory promises of Captain Quille is complete. The improvement in their daily food keeps them quiet for the moment and also gives them something to talk about.

De Gaulle to-night has made a striking and dignified speech, calling once more to the Navy, the Air Force and our Colonies, and with a personal appeal to the generals commanding in Indo-China, Syria, Algeria, Morocco—Catroux, Mittelhauser, Nogues, etc.—beseeching them to defend every particle of French soil. It was a moving speech and came from a burning heart.

Pétain has replied to him—weak words with no lofty message, the joint effort of a parliamentary palaver. To de Gaulle's noble thoughts, he offers nothing but the poor and commonplace comparison of a peasant toiling in his field although a hail-storm be falling. Can one compare the disaster of our beloved land to a simple hail-storm of no consequence? The Marshal's voice is pitiful; it is the voice of an old man, slightly senile, reading with difficulty a badly-written text prepared by the village school-master.

Bordeaux has been declared a neutral zone for a few days; just time enough for these parliamentary gentlemen to take up their quarters elsewhere, at their choice. The Germans kindly allow them to do so. Hitler is no fool; he knows how to reduce to less than nothing those who might be harmful to him, but he preserves those who may be useful to help him to beat down his enemies. He knows that a Government that has capitulated is the best agent of dissolution in France; it is therefore his natural ally in the accomplishment of his work of murder, of breaking the power of the Navy, the Air Force, the Colonies, the Armies of the Levant and Morocco. Small wonder that he is considerate to it; no German troops round Bordeaux in order not to hurt the feelings of these gentlemen and their 'ladies'. 'And the next thing to do, Gentlemen, is to choose your abode where you will be able the better to work for me.'

27 *June* 1940. Major Retel, officer commanding No. 4 Motor Depôt, visits our quarters at Rimons. He tells me that he has given me four days C.B. for having taken an ambulance two days ago, and leaving quarters without permission. His conversation with me is very friendly; he says that he understands the high motive that inspired me, that he is sympathetic to my views, but being the senior officer, he must, since he was told of my departure, inflict a punishment. As a soldier, he acknowledges but one chief, Marshal Pétain, and he must, all must, obey him. He adds: 'Your four days are done, and will merely

remain on record.' I thank him, and am touched by his kind words, realizing that he, too, is heart-broken by the disaster sanctioned by the infamous armistice. I also understand Quille's embarrassment when I came back.

We do not know whether the Navy and Air Force have agreed to surrender. I should be surprised and pained to learn that they had done so. Contradictory reports circulate: some say that the Air Force has transferred itself to North Africa, and that the Navy is at Malta or in British ports; later, it is affirmed that boats laden with air supplies have put about in the Mediterranean and returned to Marseilles. It is also affirmed that the Admiral commanding Rochefort, on receiving the order to surrender, shipped on board all new and usable supplies, weighed anchor and set his course for Plymouth.

De Gaulle continues his appeals to the Navy and to our Colonies; so it is certain that they have not all sealed their fate. Hope remains.

28 *June* 1940. De Gaulle is officially recognized by the British Government as head of all the French on British soil and in her Colonies and Dominions. He must therefore be able to recruit troops. Hurrah! A French Canadian General made a fine speech on the wireless, full of fire. He stated that in spite of the shameful armistice, Great Britain and Canada will save France. England is bristling with guns; it is not its own defence that worries Eden, but the offensive that must soon be undertaken against Germany. May his words come true!

Stuttgart is furious to-night; in spite of our sadness, we are forced to laugh uproariously at the heavy sarcasms put over, at the expense of de Gaulle, Paul Reynaud and that Jew, Mandel, who, at least, had the courage to take sides with the British. I have never admired Paul Reynaud, whom, wrongly perhaps, I have always considered a political opportunist. But if he has the guts that he seemed to express in his message to Roosevelt, he is better than his reputation; in any case, he and Mandel (whom I have always taken to be an energetic, able and honest man) have had the courage not to yield to the savage enemy.

Petrol, always petrol

Let us forget the past with its gossip; the main thing is to stand shoulder to shoulder.

If the Germans are so certain of victory, why this foaming at the mouth? Let them invade England, we'll see what they can do. The British announce a landing on the German coast, without losses to them; they brought back prisoners and killed some troops. Their Air Force continues to destroy stocks of petrol. Petrol, always petrol; will it decide the war?

29 June 1940. During lunch, someone declared that the French fleet had surrendered. My neighbour, Lieutenant Rouselle, one of our best men, turned pale and muttered between his teeth: 'If that is so, France has sunk terribly low.'

The next rumour we hear is that the Germans have invaded Spain and that their motorized columns are received enthusiastically. Indignation flares up; that's the ransom Germany exacts for her help to Franco. Her next step will be to occupy the Portuguese coast to tighten the continental blockade of Great Britain, then attack Gibraltar from the land. I refuse to swallow this last suggestion; if Germany wanted to attack Gibraltar, I argue, as we are prepared to grant her all she wants, she would have occupied the Pyrenean frontier as far as Port-Vendres and would have followed the Mediterranean coast. But the moral collapse of some of our officers is so great, that they imagine that Gibraltar, which they do not know, will be taken in a few hours' fighting by the German planes and tanks. It is quite useless for me to explain its geographical situation by land, the ease with which it can be defended, the extreme difficulty of attacking it, the underground casemates stocked with ammunition, its great guns, even its air force. No use! We, who had the best army in the world were beaten in a few weeks; no further resistance is possible.

These poor fellows, who however fought as bravely as anyone else, have received such a shock that they are still stunned, and have no sheet-anchor of hope. They are like shipwrecked men immediately after the catastrophe, drifting helplessly on a raft, dazed, nerves gone, no guiding light. But let our Allies have the smallest success, or our enemies the least check, the light will shine forth, warmer and clearer than ever. For me, the light is de Gaulle.

Discontent with our want of organization often shows now in conversation and you hear people say: 'We're fed up with continual muddling. We are fed up with the lack of organization of our High Command which has meant death to us.' Sudden outbursts of people embittered by the rancour of defeat, because they certainly preferred a hundred times more to live in what they call 'our disorder' instead of under the whip of the Nazi brutes.

Naturally, the idea of a dictatorship in France, for the moment at least, is in the minds of both officers and men. Literally I have never met a single one of my poilus who has not expressed his disgust for the parliamentary régime and has not insisted on the Deputies and their policy as being solely responsible for the disaster. These people express their thoughts inadequately. Being sincerely democratic they feel that democracy has been distorted by the misuse of the last thirty to forty years of our parliamentary government, they are so profoundly attached to the Republic, so accustomed to make use of their deputy, that when they return home, they will write him for a grant of money to rebuild their houses or in order to get a job on the railways. It is therefore the form of the democracy which must be modified. We must give back to the people the habits of high thinking, we must make them understand again the necessity and the joys of sacrifice for the common good and the Motherland.

30 *June* 1940. The church overflows with the number of men at High Mass at 11 o'clock. More than 60 per cent of our men are present, many others stand at the doors.

The weather is beautiful and calm, but our men are terribly bored. No convoying to be done. Yesterday seven lorries transported men from la Reole to the Camp de Sauge at Langnon, to the west of Bordeaux. Hardly had we entered the occupied zone when our lorries were seized by the Germans, but they were kind enough to leave us one to take back our drivers!

Some of our men take to working in the fields on the small

farms; others laze around gossiping. The go-to-bed-earlies eternally argue with the go-to-bed-lates, the latter wake up the former and vice versa; the discussion becomes heated; unconsciously they fabricate personal views which spread abroad as official news. Some play at cards from morning till night; others, to kill time, carve walking-sticks. How many wasted working days! What slackness in high places! In the neighbourhood there are some stone quarries; why not give our men a small wage and set them to extract the stone, or to deepen the ditches at the road side or to clear away the undergrowth in some of the woods, etc.? I suggest all that; I am told that they have no orders, that one must wait—always wait. Wait for what? Nothing....

The Germans were right this evening when they said that the French were doing nothing, and that they, despite their continual advance, had found time to milk stray cows. Alas! they know us well. The fact is that the High Command has made the men waste a lot of their time during the eight months preceding the attack. In 1914–18 we had to fight from the beginning. I remember that we worked like beasts of burden; even when we returned from the trenches for a rest, the work of constructing other trenches had to be carried on as soon as one arrived at the billets. And so it went on until one returned to the front line. This persistent hard work seemed natural to everybody; so when the Boche attacked, the men were fighting fit and able to make the extra effort demanded of them.

This time the same should have happened; the spirit of our soldiers, their patriotism was the same, but as soon as a man kicked and said that he was fed-up, anxiety could be read on the officers' faces, and work was quickly stopped.

1 *July* 1940. The refugees from the occupied zone can, it appears, return to their homes. My sister, who was evacuated to the Cher, will perhaps return to Paris. Did she remain in the Cher at the time of the German invasion? I have had no news of her or of anyone else.

We begin to experience difficulties in feeding our men. The

Quartermaster's Department is badly off for provisions; we are forced to live on the country-side. There are few cattle, hardly any potatoes. Wine alone is abundant and cheap.

The Zone Commander establishes controls at the approaches to every village, to check traffic. Not before it was needed, for in France, as in Belgium, during every phase of the battle, people came and went—the fifth column like the rest—freely, without let or hindrance. The real motive, perhaps, is to restrict the consumption of petrol, for we shall be short of it. Even before the war the Germans controlled the use of private cars in Germany, all fuel being reserved for the Army and the public services. The motor industry as regards private cars is dead in France, so long as the Germans remain.

The great factories (Renault, Citroen) will perhaps repair German machines; they may even make new cars, but garages selling petrol and factories making private cars will be forced to close down.

3 *July* 1940. This period of waiting makes our men very irritable. I assemble them and explain why demobilization is so slow; the lack of road and rail transport; the fact that the Germans won't allow us any petrol. It is better to speak to them frankly; they understand me and I feel that they are more composed. I profit by this change of mood to suggest reasons for hope; the petrol that the Germans use must come from Rumania or Russia; the latter power may come in on our side— there is nothing impossible in that, for Stalin must fear that once our fate and Great Britain's is settled, Hitler will turn on him—and in a few months Germany, without motor fuel, would be on her knees. Twenty thousand pilots are being trained in Canada and Australia, and if America and Great Britain can provide them with machines, the situation will be reversed, Germany and her armies will be crushed. Let us forget our old petty grievances against the English; any nation which fights the enemy is our ally, and to her our hearts go out. I am cheered by the fact that two N.C.O.s have just been to talk with me in confidence. They want to know if I can tell them of any way of getting to England to serve de Gaulle. They know that I also am

itching to go. Some thirty of their men will follow suit at the first opportunity. I tell them what I myself intend doing; we exchange addresses and promise to give each other all information we can get and to help each other mutually.

I hear from their officer that these two brave lads, in good posts in civilian life, remained to the end at Dunkirk, going through every house to find food for their company. One morning, their comrades embarked without them. Four of their men swam out to a wrecked ship which was partly above water, and succeeded in launching a life-boat. Forty men clambered into this beneath a hail of bombs, and away they rowed for a whole day and night, guided solely by a faulty compass. The next morning they discovered with terror that they were off Calais. Half dead with fatigue, they finally reached England, landing at Ramsgate after rowing for more than thirty hours.

And now, calm, resolute, clear-eyed, these two men and their company once more wish to make the journey over sea in order to continue the fight. Ah! If only I could speak freely with the men, heart to heart, and if I had the means, I would take some volunteers to de Gaulle.

The British, they say, have entered Turkey. Another false rumour surely, like the entry of the Germans into Spain, and so many others.

We are rather startled; our friend Dagommer saw, twice during the day, the motorized artillery of the innumerable German columns returning northwards from the direction of Spain, whither they had gone three days before. Something good has taken place? Do even the Germans order, counter-order and make false moves? This meagre bit of information brings a ray of hope to every soul. I knew it; at the slightest provocation, the light would shine out more clearly, more bravely.

De Gaulle, in this evening's broadcast, puts us on our guard against the sinister parody that the Vichy clowns are about to present in view of a new constitution to be imposed on France, probably under control and upon demand of the enemy. It is true that in the light of present events, our Parliament, whose mandate has in the meantime expired, does not any more represent the country's opinion; it seems probable that in the case of fresh elections most of the Deputies would lose their seats. They therefore have not the slightest right to impose any change of our political régime upon the country. In any case the Chamber of Deputies as well as the Senate voted as patriots for the declaration of war, and have since then continued to vote for the pursuance of the war and the intensification of the war effort. Neither have they been consulted about the armistice and its acceptance. Pétain has simply placed before them an accomplished fact and, now that resistance is impossible, appears to have assembled them only to help him in playing a grim comedy round the death-bed of France in agony. Nothing can now be done in France without German consent and everything they ask must be done. So what happens? One is dumbfounded in thinking of the rôle Pétain is playing. De Gaulle is right in warning us. How humiliating to think that Hitler has found a French Marshal that he can order about, that Pétain has to beg a Goebbels or a Goering to approve his speeches. Pétain! Who would have thought it!

The wireless states this evening that Weygand has gone to Syria to bring about the capitulation of Mittelhauser's fine army without a fight. Mittelhauser is considered to be a great Frenchman, will he capitulate? He can, he must take his army to Palestine, to Egypt, or better still, remain where he is to defend the oil of Irak and keep Syria for us.

Do Pétain and Weygand think that Great Britain is incapable both of defending herself and of winning the war with her 500,000,000 subjects, her unlimited powers of purchasing arms from America, and her Dominions who have thrown themselves body and soul into the struggle? Perhaps they do; but others, de Gaulle, revealed to us a few weeks ago as the ace of aces, Admiral Muselier, his representative for the Navy, Paul Reynaud, Mandel, a man of great intelligence, think the opposite. These are the men to inspire our confidence. I suspect Pétain and Weygand of having been imposed upon by the pack of politicians who during the last twenty years have never done the right thing in any circumstance whatever. Their past in no wise guarantees the present.

Captain Quille, who with his brothers, runs a large public

works contractor's business in the north, confirms what I have always thought: that our anti-tank defences, ditches, upright railway metals, etc., were futile. He tells me that he demonstrated this to all the staff officers of the 1st Army to which he and I belonged. He himself was attached to the General Staff.

At his own expense he sent for mechanical diggers as used for large earthworks (for digging canals and ports, levelling banks, etc.). They are mounted on caterpillars with hoists and levelling apparatus. The machine had first to cross a network of rails planted vertically. It grabbed the rails, a pull on a lever and they were twisted and knocked down like straws. Next the caterpillar, furnished with what I think is called a 'bulldozer', tackled an anti-tank ditch. It dropped its 'bulldozer' like a sort of mobile bridge, in different directions; then it flattened out the anti-tank ditch and passed over. The whole business, timed by staff officers with watch in hand, took three minutes.

Quille proved, as he said he would: (1) that the defences were ridiculous; (2) that it was only necessary to fit a certain number of tanks with 'bulldozers' to enable them to cross the defences erected by our enemies. He made a long report based on the experiment carried out in the Valenciennes-Maubeuge sector where the enemy attacked and penetrated into France, thus breaking our line of resistance. His report was pigeon-holed, without even being considered. Appalling!

4 *July* 1940.   Great news on the wireless! The British fleet has captured our fleet assembled at Mers-el-Kébir near Oran, under the command of Admiral Gensoul. A few ships tried to escape, in particular the *Dunkerque*. The British shelled and sank it. They announce that the majority of the ships are now at Gibraltar or on their way to England. It is pathetic that we and the British have come to this. But one must believe that most of the ships resisted merely for form's sake, and are really glad not to have to lie in our ports completely at the mercy of the Italians and Germans.

I know only too well the splendid spirit of officers and ratings who, scorning and hating Italian sailors, harbour feelings of age-long friendship and respect for the valour of British seamen whom they have met on the seven seas.

The English Admiral wanted to get the French fleet away from the clutches of the Germans and Italians and suggested to Admiral Gensoul that it should proceed to Martinique, where it could be disarmed far beyond the reach of our enemies. This was an honourable proposal, which should have been accepted if our enemies, as they claim, had no intention of grabbing our fleet to use it one day against the British.

Gensoul wirelessed the French Government for instructions which had to be obtained from the new master, Hitler. Receiving the order to refuse, it seems to me he just made a show of fighting and flight.

Officers and men, listening to Stuttgart and Rome, roared with laughter when the speakers angrily declared that Churchill should have confidence in the word of two men who had never lied—Hitler and Mussolini. That is a tall one! What about Austria, Czecho-Slovakia, Poland and Albania?

5 *July* 1940. The German and Italian wireless rave and storm about the capture of the French fleet at Mers-el-Kébir. Well! Well! Why get so worked up about it if they had no intention of using our vessels? It would seem as though the blow has hit them in a tender spot.

How can anyone be so simple as to imagine that once the fleet had been disarmed and anchored at Toulon, that the Boche and those born cheats the Italians would not have picked some quarrel on the pretext that we had violated the armistice terms in some way or other and by way of reprisal take possession of the fleet which would be at their mercy? All very well, Hitler, but you can't go on fooling everybody all the time.

The Germans make the most of the incident and try to embroil us with the English; but this does not alter the fact that French hopes are centred on England and we are delighted to see our fleet continuing the fight for the common cause under the Union Jack.

The Boches read us a long batch of articles from Bulgarian, Hungarian and Chinese papers which are in their pay, condemning the British action. The English read us articles from the leading American papers highly commending their act of prudence.

I prefer the American opinion to that of unknown rags from Budapest or Sofia. A matter of taste!

As for the French newspapers, on Government instructions, under the heel and perhaps in the pay of our enemies, they condemn the British action, but often in comparatively mild terms.

The French press no longer exists. It no longer has the right to publish the English communiqués, nor to relate any bold feat of arms by our troops, nor to publish any articles which could revive the morale of the country. It must not speak of our defeat and abasement, nor of the hard times ahead. It must keep us beaten and dejected, persuade us there is no hope, turn the knife in the wound which must not be allowed to heal up, dissipate any idea of revenge and of possible English victory, try to turn us against them and who knows, perhaps, arm us one day against our ally. But above all they must keep us in the stupor and torpor of the hopelessly vanquished. That probably is the 'New Order' so noisily promised by Hitler and Mussolini. But not for me, thank you.

6 *July* 1940. No more talk about the dismemberment of Rumania by Russia. It is interesting however; the Russians are one day's march from the oil wells, Germany will be at her mercy for motor spirit, since Russia has already taken the Galician oil field. In 24 hours they can deprive Hitler of petrol. Will they? All the cards have not yet been played....

The British have bombed the wreck of the *Dunkerque* stranded at Mers-el-Kébir to make sure that she cannot be refloated. Bravo!

Jean Prouvost, always ready to sell himself to anyone, is now chief of propaganda. He lied in most barefaced fashion over the wireless, saying: 'This is how the English have repaid the help given by the French navy at Dunkirk, help which enabled them to save four-fifths of the British Army, whilst we were only able to save half of ours.'

England and the Pétain Government

When I embarked, I only saw British warships which on that day were convoying vessels loaded with French and English troops. The master of the cargo-boat that I was on told me that each of his trips to Dunkirk had been under the protection of the British Navy. Certainly our Navy also assisted with the embarkation and the protection of the shipping, but to a lesser degree. That is quite intelligible, if you consider the number of British and French warships available in the North Sea at that time.

But Jean Prouvost had to submit his text to the Boches before reading it at the microphone and this lie was probably heartily approved by Goebbels. What a dirty dog. He wound up with a pun, saying that the English, to thank us for Dunkirk, had bombed the *Dunkerque*. Feeble !

The French Government announced, after the attack at Mers-el-Kébir, that they had broken off diplomatic relations with England. They blundered, however, by adding that English diplomatic representatives had been withdrawn from France ten days ago. It was, therefore, the English Government and not ours which broke off diplomatic relations. We merely confirmed the decision of London to have no further dealings with the Pétain Government which was not recognized as a free government; it has given too many proofs of the contrary and continues to show it from day to day.

The French Government, obeying orders from Berlin, tries to discredit de Gaulle and Admiral Muselier. De Gaulle is said to have been condemned by court-martial to four years imprisonment for going to England, and Admiral Muselier had previously been dismissed from the service for insubordination and lack of principle. A vile proceeding, which stinks of the Boche !

But the Government forgets to tell how de Gaulle, in command of a division, was mentioned in despatches by Weygand in June, and was described as 'a spirited and bold leader who attacked the bridgehead at Abbeville strongly held by the enemy. He broke the German resistance and advanced 9 miles into the enemy lines, taking hundreds of prisoners and bringing back a considerable quantity of material and equipment.' That certainly is a bit awkward for Pétain and Weygand.

The German jack-boot

Meanwhile de Gaulle and Muselier are not doing too badly. They continue to encourage us with their bold speeches, full of dash and so virile after the bitter and circumlocutory utterances of our so-called government. The numerous, daily communiqués concerning refugees, demobilization, resumption of work, etc. are full of items and hidden meanings which destroy the preceding information, the sentences are so twisted and ambiguous that you can't make anything of them. Never a definite order, statement or indication. Now from bitter to sweet. A masterpiece which shows the interest of the Marshal's government in the country, the refugees and the troops eagerly awaiting their demobilization: the wireless announces the resumption of train services on certain sections of the railway: Vichy-Marseilles, Vichy-Nimes, Vichy-Bordeaux. That's all! Vichy—because the government is summoning Parliament to confirm the great reform of the constitution which they impose on the country—with German approval, you may be sure.

Members at the double, to vote! But that the refugees may return home, together with the hundreds of thousands of troops, fed and paid, kept in idleness and not demobilized for want of transport: Hell, what does that matter, it's merely a damn nuisance. This haste on the part of the Vichy Government is very suspicious. Is it not in order to impose upon the country an adulterated constitution before demobilizing the army and sending the men home, where, relatively freer, they might protest against the bitter pill they will have to swallow? That is of the utmost importance. When the ill deed had been done, then we will see about the demobilization and repatriation of refugees.

Yes, something has changed in France. We had our political battles before. People fought with voting-papers, in order to beat their opponents during elections. To-day, when one should fight against the Boche, a French Marshal assembles Parliament with undue haste, so that we may receive, without offering any resistance, the 'coup de grâce' from the enemy.

Good God! whither are we going! De Gaulle to the rescue. Imagine feeling and seeing all that and allowing criminal hands to cut our throats, rob us and roll us in the mire without being able to cry out 'Thief', 'Murder'; how we inwardly rage!

Delay in demobilization

A wave of excessive severity is spreading in the higher command. Colonel Leonard de Juvigny, in command of the Gironde area, has just given Captain Quille two days close arrest because he gave the motor cyclist despatch-rider of the depôt a pass valid for five days instead of signing one daily. Quille has been locked up in the cells at the town hall of la Réole, like a criminal; a plate of stew was taken to him without knife and fork and spoon, so that he had to eat with his fingers. Quille got the Military Cross and two 'mentions' in the last war! Why this useless severity?

From the very beginning of the campaign complete freedom was accorded to road transport on duty, but now we no longer have the right to go from one village to the next. During the fighting in Belgium and France it would certainly have paid to be strict, particularly as the fifth columnists were travelling about as freely as in peace time. When it was a question of movement under shell fire in Belgium or at Dunkirk, we were not pestered for passes and signatures; but now this excessive and unwarranted severity provokes bitter comment among the officers.

Colonel Leonard de Juvigny, who has a hook in place of his left arm, lost in the last war, was passing a few days ago through a village and came upon some soldiers who were playing in a jazz band for want of something better to do. He stopped his car and, rushing among them knocked their instruments out of their hands and stamped on them, then turning on the men, he tore and slashed their clothing with his formidable hook, swore at them and got back to his car, leaving the poor fellows thunderstruck by this unexpected attack. Present events must have turned his head a bit.

As to spies, the commonest disguise apparently was a priest's cassock or a nun's robe, over the uniform. In the Rouen area some hundreds were arrested—and shot, I hope.

10 *July* 1940. Inaction; demobilization is proceeding very slowly except for the troops from the unoccupied zone, all of whom should be home by the end of the month. For the occupied zone the Government is trying to come to terms with the Germans. But the Germans claim that it is the French Govern-

ment which is delaying the demobilization . . . certain categories will be released: farmers, the older men and employees of public services.

The most contradictory rumours are abroad as to German methods regarding fit men in the occupied zone; sometimes they are requisitioned for public works; sometimes rounded up into labour camps; on the other hand, they are occasionally left absolutely free. This uncertainty calms the impatience of the men a bit, as above all they dread the idea of a labour camp.

14 *July* 1940. (*Sunday.*)   There are many troops at Mass and after the service I parade them and march them in column to the neighbouring war memorial where I tell them the reasons for hope in spite of the present mourning of the Motherland. We have one minute's silence in homage to the dead of the last war and of this. Then I lead the column to the open space before the town hall over which a large tricolour is floating. There we all sing the Marseillaise. What enthusiasm and emotion I feel amongst these men! I dismiss the parade after calling for three cheers for France, hands raised to the flag as though taking an oath of faithfulness and vengeance. It seems that for a moment the fires of the spirit have been rekindled.

The first men to be demobilized, the older farmers, will go home to-morrow.

De Gaulle often speaks to us in the evenings, but you have to try a number of different wave-lengths, as the Germans jam some of them so badly that you cannot make anything of it. If the French people pay no heed to de Gaulle's appeals, as the Berlin wireless maintains, why trouble to jam his broadcasts and the English communiqués which daily advise us of the destruction of factories in Germany by their planes?

The German communiqués give an impressive figure of English merchant shipping which has been sunk; if they are telling the truth and continue at the same rate, it will cause the British some uneasiness. But is it correct?

16 *July* 1940.   The new French Government has been elected amid general indifference. What has been changed? Nothing,

in fact, since its formation. The chief prepossession seems to be the nomination of Secretaries of State, but demobilization remains slow. We do not understand why the Germans should seek to hinder men from returning to the fields and factories; isn't it to their own interest that we should start again to produce our own food? Is the Government trying to keep together a mass of troops in the unoccupied zone with a view to eventual action against the Germans, if their campaign against Britain fails? The whole thing is a mystery. Personally I believe it is due to the congenital paralysis of the Government, which is composed of spineless politicians and as incapable of any action as ever.

20 *July* 1940. It is nearly a month now since the armistice was signed and we haven't yet got rid of a fifth of our men. Yet we are comparatively lucky, for since the armistice we have received quite a batch of men belonging to the neighbourhood of Montpellier who have been able to return home as this is in the unoccupied zone. In the occupied zone only the older farmers, civil servants (naturally), and employees in the public services have been sent back. The men are fed up and downhearted. We have done some odd jobs for the district council: made a road across the fields between two hamlets, cleaned out an old washing place silted up by the rains. But the mayor, Monsieur Beausoleil (the right name for the south), has nothing more for us to do. It has been raining daily for eight days.

Between storms and showers I go for long walks in this pretty and hilly countryside, where you can find lovely woods, Lombardy poplars, cedars, streams bordered by willows gleaming in the breeze and the sun, where the meadows and vines alternate with fields of tobacco, maize, and corn. I like the church steeple, inspired by Greek lines and surmounted by the cross; the bells, which sound so clearly in the pure morning air, can be clearly seen; the adjoining cemetery is planted with gloomy cypresses which stand out boldly in the clear air. What a delightful range of colours through all the varying greens and yellows. From my window I have a view over a pretty little valley richly green, thanks to the recent rain, where clumps of trees are dotted about as in a fine park; yokes of white oxen are slowly drawing little carts, or blue-green tanks for sulphating (to kill blight, etc. on the vines) or a plough of the same model as those employed by the Romans over a thousand years ago. The friendly, cultivated inhabitants express themselves with ease, and frequently with a delicacy which shows their ancient culture.

Can it be that France has had her day like Athens, Rome, Spain or Portugal in the past? Is it Germany's turn now? No. Our virtues and our culture, which only twenty years ago proved so strong and full of life, have not been killed by a mere handful of politicians. Amongst our Deputies and Senators, there were quite a lot of honest people, but the wrong application of the parliamentary system paralysed their good intentions. Rebuild the Republic; that is the post-war programme. Fundamentally the people are alright. I know them too well, our soldiers, peasants, workers, and middle-class shop-keepers. I know that the country has not changed. They are the true face of France, and as soon as the enemy shows signs of weakening, all of them will rush to attack him, to drive him out of France, with the same frenzy as of twenty years ago.

Hitler has made a speech to the Reichstag and the wireless has translated some passages for us. He affects calm, the tone of a conqueror sure of his power. His unheard-of successes to the day and hour are proof of his invincible power, he says. Well, Napoleon said the same thing for ten years; yet he had his Waterloo. Hitler says that the war doesn't interest him: he merely wants to reorganize Europe on the lines of his plan. Perhaps, but why doesn't he tell us about this plan, which is to bring happiness to us and to all European peoples? Wouldn't this be the best way of winning to this European cause all the vanquished: Austrians, Czechs, Poles, Norwegians, French and others: and also the English? Why not? If he does not divulge this before enslaving us, it can only be because his plan would be unacceptable to free nations. His silence confirms our fears. It is already announced that the money of the future will not be based on gold. Europe will have her currencies and above them all will be the Reichmark, the money of the master-race; the other peoples will have the currency of slave-races.

Meanwhile all we have from him is war, misfortune, murder

and ruin. You may be sure this will be solely a German plan; the rest of us will be outcasts, compelled to sweat blood under the lash to produce guns, tanks and planes.

But neither the English nor we are vanquished or slaves. What a pity the U.S.A. are so slow to understand things; they will get a sad awakening. Hitler announces that he will make total war upon Britain if his offer is refused; France, the only military power capable of offering some resistance to Germany, was beaten in a month; England will only be a mouthful. If that is so, why doesn't he get on with it? Why call upon them to surrender without fighting, if he is sure of winning in a few weeks? Up to the present he has not been particular about shedding the blood of his troops or of his opponents. But getting across the Channel is not quite the same thing as crossing the Sambre or the Seine. That is where Napoleon came to grief.

And naturally he says, as in the case of Poland and Czecho-Slovakia, that if England does not yield to his threats she will be responsible for the war which will rage upon her soil, just like the apache who threatens a man with a revolver and says: 'Your money or your life.'

Hitler always endeavours by the same methods first of all to separate the nations from each other, and then to divide the peoples against their governments. He is trying, therefore, with the assistance of the fifth column which he has recruited in England, and elsewhere, to make trouble with the faint-hearted by picturing Great Britain as led by the nose by international Jewish finance. But the English are too patriotic, too deeply attached to their soil, to their liberties, their King and their Empire to be duped by a liar who has never once honoured his word or his signature.

21 *July* 1940. A new wireless station in Paris, Boche, without a doubt, is giving some rather curious broadcasts. Using very cunning arguments, it is furiously attacking the Vichy Government, deriding its inaction and its failure to arrange the demobilization of the army. 'What are your ministers doing? Nothing. What need have you of any ministers who make you pay dearly and are incapable of any action? Men with the

forces, you should be home by now; why don't you go?...'
Hitler is right, but his obvious aim is to divide us and win us over
to Hitlerism, which alone is capable of organizing and governing.
He rouses doubts in many minds.

This station largely broadcasts the articles of a new paper,
The Pillory, actually inspired by the Germans and always calling for Draconian measures against Freemasons and Jews.

It is a clever move. I can hear some of my best comrades
saying: 'Bravo, if he rids us of the Jews and Freemasons, that
will be something gained at any rate. We should never get rid of
them without him.'

Hitler is employing the same method as in Germany, the old
method recommended by Machiavelli: to league the people
against a common enemy. Formerly the radicals set us against
the Church whilst they ruled for thirty years. To-day Hitler is
leaguing French people against the Jew and the Freemason.
Thence it is but a step for the shallow-minded and sectarian to
look upon him as a saviour. Considering that he represents
England as governed by the same Jewish, Communist conspiracy, it is only another step to turn us against her and enrol
us as soldiers in the great crusade of purification.

If we really want to reform anything here, we'll do it after the
victory of de Gaulle and the British. And we'll do it as Frenchmen and not as Hitler's flunkeys.

22 *July* 1940. To-day we have information about the swin-
dling methods of the Germans in occupied territory, thanks to the
special marks with which their troops are furnished to be spent
only in France. The soldiers get 2 marks or 40 francs per day;
they buy quantities of goods, principally lingerie and ladder-
proof silk stockings and such like, which they post to their wives.
Our shops are stripped bare for scraps of paper of no value. The
draper who receives these very doubtful marks loses no time in
paying the butcher and the baker with them, and they in turn
pass them as promptly to their customers. By virtue of the
well-known rule, 'Bad money drives out good', the French
banknotes are hoarded up and more and more of the Germans
scraps of paper circulate.

German officers and men buy champagne, rich wines, etc. and pay with their wretched paper.

A refugee told me that in the village of St Amand-de-Boixe, in the Charente, there were a number of refugees from the Moselle ardently pro-French before the disaster. But as soon as the Germans came, they rushed to their cars. The women got in the officers' cars and pointed out the houses where they could find accommodation and what people should be turned out to make room for them. They spent the evening with the Germans at the café. When it is announced that refugees are to report at the Kommandatur, it is always specified 'except those from the Moselle' who are looked upon as already having returned to the Reich. Moreover, they and the Alsatians have been allowed to return home without formalities.

It is reported from Angoulême that a man was sentenced to a fine of 10,000 francs and six months' imprisonment for listening to the English wireless. But a German soldier arrested for stealing a wallet has been shot.

If you utter the word 'Boche', 800 francs fine on the spot, etc.

This is the sort of régime promised to those who are so weak as to remain under the jack-boot, not to speak of labour camps in France and perhaps in Germany and Poland; for the London wireless announces that the Germans have already collected 50,000 Belgians who have been sent like cattle to Germany.

23 *July* 1940. London advises us that French pilots serving in England have bombed Germany. They are brave men, for the Germans have announced that any Frenchman taken prisoner whilst fighting for the British will be considered as a franc-tireur and shot immediately. But we have plenty of bold fellows.

24 *July* 1940. The first bold and useful act of the French Government has been to abolish the privilege of possessing private stills, the privilege which for thirty years has marred and depopulated our finest provinces and killed more men, women and children than three wars would have done. Everyone agreed that to allow this to persist was a crime against the nation, but the privilege was 'taboo', since fear of the electors made our

miserable Deputies more cowardly on this question than on any
other.

25 *July* 1940.   Major Jacquemard, officer in charge of the
canton of Monségur, has entrusted me with the grouping together in two parks of the 1300 odd motor transport vehicles
stationed about the district.   Quickly I arrange squads of men to
receive and classify the vehicles: cars, small lorries, lorries,
buses, tractors, caterpillars, etc.; squads of mechanics to put in
hand urgent repairs, and also clerks to make out and fill in as the
transport arrives the countless reports, lists, and other papers
which have to be produced at every turn.   Hard work, interesting and absorbing for a few days; all these machines, of which
many are quite new, arrive from all directions from seven in the
morning until seven at night.   I manage to avoid any congestion, and everything passes off well.

I chatted to-day with the father of one of our drivers who has
come from Rouen.   In a hotel, he says, where German officers
have installed their mess, one of them, a few days ago, asked his
fellows to stand for a minute's silence to honour the memory of
some of their men who had been sent by motor-boat to reconnoitre the English coasts.   Not one had returned. This man
states that the Germans are increasing their attempts to find out
the weak spots in the English coastal defences, but they all fail.
Some of them are no longer able to conceal their terror at having
to undertake these expeditions.

A few days before that, he added, about fifty German planes
were reported to have been destroyed on the ground at an
aerodrome near Rouen by British aircraft.

From various sources I learn that numbers of German women
and children are coming to France; they say that their towns
are becoming untenable because of the British bombing raids.
These Hun women are at Bordeaux, Langon and Paris.   Hamburg, Hanover, and the Rhineland have particularly suffered.
Furthermore, the German wireless, which until now has always
maintained that British bombing has been without effect, now
denounces to the world their enemies' misdeeds in bombing and
destroying numbers of hamlets, villages and towns, killing civi-

lians, women and children. Well! Who started it? Who machine-gunned French villages and long lines of refugees? Who was it who disembowelled dozens of women around the bomb craters on the road to Lille? It happened too in Poland, as it would happen in England. This British aviation, which they daily ridicule, can't be so insignificant. This evening there is a change in their tone. The Germans will perhaps have to do a bit of thinking; they will learn that not everything in the garden is lovely.

26 *July* 1940.   Captain Quille has managed to get demobilized and has departed. From the 15th, I could have done likewise, but I am waiting to see my sister before setting out on my travels.

Demobilization is incomprehensibly slow; the Germans make a show of not offering any opposition, and throw the responsibility on our Government, whose problems are legion. Nothing goes forward, neither the demobilization, nor the return of the refugees, nor the reorganization of the country. The newspapers only publish long lists of Secretaries of State, prefects, ambassadors, and civil servants—of useful measures, none whatsoever! The job-finding Republic has started work again.

The German wireless announces that one of their submarines has sunk the French troopship, the *Mecknès*, loaded with 1300 men repatriated from England. They throw the responsibility for the 'incident'—fine word—on the British, who didn't warn them. When the Germans sink a ship with 1300 French soldiers, it is an 'incident'. When the British kill two hundred sailors at Mers-el-Kébir, it is an unforgettable crime. Unforgettable? Possibly, but no one speaks of the two to three hundred thousand French soldiers, women, children, old men, who were wounded or killed during the war on the roads and in the villages. That is probably forgotten, but the French must never forget the two hundred sailors killed at Mers-el-Kébir.

27 *July* 1940.   I was very glad to meet one of my old sergeants, Michel, who went through the whole campaign with me. He is at Réole, and I was unaware of it. He is demobilized, but

he delayed his departure in order to cycle over to see me, in spite of the awful heat. The poor fellow was bathed in sweat. I invited him to lunch. He and a good part of his company spent six days in an English camp near Southampton. He told me in detail what a marvellous reception they had. All the men had new uniforms, splendid footwear, linen, etc. Sixty Gillette razors were distributed among them. A Colonel invited him and thirty poilus to a garden-party; cigarettes on entering, tea, cakes. The Red Cross also invited all our men to a party. Each received a shilling to spend at the booths, and still more cigarettes, cakes, iced drinks, presents and souvenirs. In camp, tennis-players had only to ask for balls and rackets, and they were supplied. Everyone received embarkation allowance: 5s. for the men, 15s. for the N.C.O.s, £1 for the officers and English rate of pay while in England. They were literally brothers in arms. Do I hear you say that all that was pre-arranged, all those presents from private people, that enthusiasm, the generosity of those patriotic and charitable societies? What nonsense! Those actions came from the heart; they were not the result of commands. It was just the same for my companions and myself during our rapid transit through England after Dunkirk.

A month later they would have us believe that the British are our enemies; that they consider us to be mercenary, that they despise us and have betrayed us by not giving us all the help possible. Wretched lies!

Every Frenchman knows a soldier who fought in Flanders and has returned via England; let him ask how he was received there and if he brought back a kindly memory. Let him ask too if he was not struck by the order, the discipline, the cleanliness and the good manners to be found everywhere. Alas! The Boches are not the only nation to combine order and method; I hope these gentlemen will find that out one day.

29 *July* 1940. Richard, one of our good drivers from the Sarthe, has received a letter from his wife, telling him that the Chateau de Soueches, in their neighbourhood and the property of the Duke des Carres, was occupied by a very important German military staff. The British reduced the castle and its

contents to dust. Five miles from there, they bombed and machine-gunned a German convoy. Our friends are not satisfied with ports and aerodromes; the fifth column in France is working for them, the Germans now having them behind them, and not in front, as before.

A day of reports which for once do not conflict. Two drivers from Brittany receive letters from home which both state that the Germans do not look forward to attacking Great Britain. They are scared of the sea and know full well that none of those who have set out on reconnaissance duties have returned. They would have to be embarked at the point of the bayonet. And Madame Rousselle,who has just arrived from Le Mans, bears out this statement when she tells us that the Germans fear having to entrain for Rennes, which is on the way to the coast from which they are to sail to England. Many German soldiers complain that they have had no home leave for more than a year. Time drags heavily for them. On all sides it is confirmed that the Germans are stripping our shops with their worthless paper money in order to send parcels home to their Gretchens.

30 *July* 1940.　Germany and Britain are engaged in a wireless bombardment of statistics proving that the other will starve this winter. I can understand Britain's attitude, for she has always predicted a long war. But Germany talks always of her lightning war, which will smash her enemy in a few weeks. Then why worry, since if the British starve this winter they will no longer exist?

Demobilization still very slow. Several of our men have managed to be demobilized at Rimons; then the Kommandatur of Sauveterre told them that they could return to their homes in Seine Inférieure without difficulties. They have gone and their friends are impatient to hear from them.

My car park goes on well; I have more than a thousand vehicles nicely lined up under the trees of the Monségur fair ground and on the sports ground.

The Germans have forbidden the transport of all mail in France, especially between occupied and non-occupied zones. Why? Is it a measure of security in case they are preparing the big offensive against Britain? We are in the dark. The absence of letters contributes to the lowering of the spirits of the men. They suffer cruelly from this imbecile and enforced idleness in which the authorities insist on keeping them.

1 *August* 1940.   At Monségur I met Second-Lieutenant Roth of my old company. He is stationed at Réole, and has come here to arrange with the gentlemen of the Privy Council who have withdrawn to this town, in order to drive them to Clermont-Ferrand. He and two N.C.O.s, in charge of a large convoy, will transport the luggage of these high personages. Moreover, the State has made a present to these gentlemen and their 'ladies'—their ladies came with them—of more than 500 gallons of petrol for their personal cars. Poor refugees are refused a mere five gallons to return to their homes. And the Privy Council's duty is to expose irregularities and abuses! These gentry realize so well how outrageous the whole action is that they discuss with Roth the spot where the 500 gallons shall be handed over to them, as they do not wish to have any trouble with the people.

2 *August* 1940.   The wireless announces that de Gaulle has been sentenced to death by a court-martial presided over by General Frère, the same general who commanded the army which was to have helped us. De Gaulle's division was a part of his army. An N.C.O. of my company, who was in de Gaulle's division, goes so far as to say that de Gaulle asked for reinforcements from General Frère for two days, in order to follow up his success, but Frère did not send them. This is perplexing. Frère was perhaps jealous of de Gaulle's successes; in any case, he is dishonoured by consenting to pronounce capital punishment on a French general who is guilty of fighting the invader in order to deliver his country. Doubtless the sentence is instigated by order of the Government, which, in its turn, obeys France's murderers. I should never have believed that a general could have been found to agree to carry out such a task. To put a brake on Frenchmen leaving to join up under de Gaulle in too great numbers, the Government has decided that all those who engage in a foreign army will be liable to the death sentence. So much

the better; those who are already there, and those who will go, will be an élite, ready for any sacrifice.

I go to Eauze in the Gers, to present my company's accounts and there, and at Castelnau D'Auzan, I find a great number of my brave poilus whom I have not seen since the English days. I had scarcely entered a café at Castelnau with a few of them, when the news of my arrival spread like a trail of gunpowder. The café quickly filled up. What a joy it was to see once more their broad beaming faces. I felt by their eyes, by their vigorous handshakes, that they were glad to see me. I spent two hours with them, with innumerable litres of white wine, listening to their tales and the news of those demobilized, and also, alas, of those killed or wounded at Dunkirk. The losses were much heavier than I had supposed, for the column that I had split up into small parties had covered a long line and it was impossible to know what was going on five or six hundred yards away in the morning twilight. Nor was I able to call the roll on the boat aboard which only a part of my men were shipped with me.

At Eauze I settle my accounts with the gallant Captain Quiqampoix, a stout fellow who went through the last war as I did. Coming from Lille, he cannot return home, so he is trying to obtain the management of a transport company or a youth camp. But (this is a little weakness of his) it must be in a large town and not in a little hole like Eauze, which is, however, a charming town in delightful country, and very hospitable.

5 *August* 1940. At Monségur I meet Pierre Masson, with whom I was very friendly for years. Life and business had separated us. His wife and daughters, whom I knew as little children, live, for the time being, on an estate half a mile from Monségur. Jacqueline, the eldest of his daughters, whom I last saw eleven years ago on the sands of Villers-sur-mer, is married to a flying officer, who has just been demobilized, and is expecting a baby in two months' time. The Massons have decided to return to Paris. For want of anything better, they have the idea of hiring a lorry to take back all the family and their luggage. To help them on the way, two of my drivers, who wish to return to Paris, will accompany them. I am able to get

them some diesel oil. Who would have predicted such an Odyssey?

7 *August* 1940. I obtain my demobilization, and intend to reach Casablanca. I'll look round there. In order to take advantage of a free passage, I must go to the camp at Lannemezan, which is, I believe, somewhere near Tarbes. There is a risk of remaining there for a long time, for troop transports to North Africa are rare. I am in haste to get on with my plan; and so, as soon as I have paid a short visit to Masson's factory at Orec, near Saint-Etienne, I shall go down to Marseilles to try and book a passage on board a mixed cargo boat bound for any port in Algeria or Morocco. I get a tailor at Monségur to make me a lounge suit—it's not at all bad. I have two suit-cases in all, one for my military effects and the other for my linen. With that I can go a long way.

8 *August* 1940. A great aero-naval battle has been fought over the south coast of England. The figures of planes brought down by the two sides present an enormous difference. You cannot even strike a decent average, so great is the difference. The British announce 59 German planes down, and in spite of the German attack they bombed aerodromes and various objectives from Ludwigshaven as far as Brest, including Dunkirk, Calais and Caen. So they do not seem to be short of aeroplanes.

I hand over the command of the car parks at Monségur to one of my officers, Lieutenant Poulain, and I will help him until I go, on 12 August, although now I am a civilian. Major Jacquemard tells me that all these vehicles were originally to be sold by auction, but now they will probably be returned to the makers, who will put them in order and will sell them gradually, as orders come in. This is an excellent solution and far preferable to the first suggestion.

Of the six or seven hundred drivers that we had with our detachment at Rimons, there remain only seventy-two, whom Poulain is to take to Monségur. Nearly all our men have been demobilized, even those who, theoretically, cannot return to their department, Paris, Seine-Inférieure, etc., that is, all those departments to the north of the Loire. These men claimed domicile in Bordeaux, Tours and other towns and they have managed to return home individually, without any difficulty. The first, at least, were successful and wrote to their friends of their safe arrival. 'The Germans', they wrote, 'not only put no difficulties in the way, but even helped us.' In short, what the Government was incapable of doing, the men did themselves without any trouble. Why? Decidedly, the more one sees and hears of the inefficient working of the personnel of the government, their speeches and their daily round of activities, the more one longs for someone to come and sweep out the Augean stables.

11 August 1940.   I take my last meal at the mess and feel sad at saying goodbye to my brother-officers, especially Chapuis and charming Rousselle. I know those who will join me and be impatiently waiting to hear of my doings.

During the day, General René Altmeyer, much decorated, came and inspected the young 1939 class. He gave them a neat little speech on one's duties to the country; he also gave one hundred francs to a lad who has eleven brothers and sisters. He had a look at the park. He's a fine man, tall and spare, with an eagle-like profile, and black, keen eyes. I saw him twice at Bray-Dunes, near Dunkirk, the day before we embarked. He, I think, took command of the defence of what remained of the Dunkirk region in order to protect the embarkation. His sharp tone, his staccato speech accompanied by energetic movements of the hands struck me at the time.

12 August 1940. (*Monday*.)   Departure at 8.30 with Pierre Masson. Lunch at Brive with Masson and his manager, who was waiting for us. The conversation is of millions of francs' worth of army orders. I am rather ashamed to hear his manager say with a shade of regret: 'If only the war had lasted a year longer, we should have made fifteen millions merely with the orders already on the books.' A warped outlook, if I may say so; the man is decent enough, was in an anti-aircraft unit and is full of admiration for his brother, a very keen pilot, and a flight-sergeant of the Regular Army, who has brought down two Messerschmitts and like many another has passed over to de Gaulle in England.

Before the town hall of Brive I see an enormous crowd listening to a shrieking loud speaker. It concerns the repatriation of the refugees; those leaving the next day are being called to receive instructions from the mayor's parlour. There are not many refugees here, and violent, but useless protests arise from the crowd. They are told what formalities are to be complied with, and where to sign on and assemble. Then the crowd disperses, exchanging angry and bitter remarks. There used to be forty trains a day, one hears, now there is only one. What is the Government doing? The Boches have taken all the trucks and railway carriages, people reply. How these simple and exasperated folk get hold of wrong information and stupid stories!

Before the town hall I also see six large wooden panels similar to those brought out at election-time on which are posted the candidates' appeals. They are covered with a multitude of small papers held in position by drawing pins. Refugees write down their names and addresses in an attempt to find lost families or to obtain news of those who have disappeared. Modest scraps of paper, heartrending appeals scrawled in pencil; sometimes it may be a mother asking for news of her lost child, or a son who has disappeared, or a husband of whom she cannot glean a word.

I sleep at the hotel of the Truffe Noire, where I have a room with every comfort, hot and cold water, a luxury that I had long ago forgotten.

15 *August* 1940. Yesterday at La Bourboule. Slept at the hotel of the same name. The manageress, a rather elderly and distinguished-looking lady, tells me that her hotel has been requisitioned for a long time past, for Deputies, important civil servants, journalists and others who now are in the Vichy Government. She is disgusted by all the intriguing, the scheming and the lying that she has seen and heard. Those people think always of themselves and never of France; not only has nothing changed, but it is worse than before, she says. To-day, Royat and Clermont-Ferrand. At Royat, nearly

all the hotels have been requisitioned for bank officials, civil servants and the Privy Council, late of Monségur. Pierre Masson is going to have a long conversation with one of the directors of the Banque de l'Union Parisienne, which is his business bank. On coming out, a M. de la Blénière accompanied him; General de Gaulle's brother, he told me, is one of his subordinates. We meet him at one of the spa-waters in the town; he gives me some information about his brother, with whom he has not been able to correspond since he left for London; also news of all his family which I will pass on to the General.

I forgot to note at Brive that some officers of the Arsenal, with whom we had an appetiser, gave us some interesting information about the way orders for armaments have been handled. Before being able to issue an order, once its necessity was accepted, three months generally elapsed in covering reams of paper; each contract had to be prepared in triplicate with the manufacturer's signature, but in the Government offices, a minimum of forty copies were made, and sometimes even sixty-five for the innumerable files, registers and departments which required them. Pierre Masson says that a small armament part was delivered by him to Hotchkiss, who checked and signed for it; Hotchkiss asked for forty copies of the invoice; thinking that there must be a mistake, he supplied four. There was no mistake, and he had to make out the rest. The officers admit that every-one wishes to safeguard himself to such an extent that the signing and execution of contracts is seriously hampered by the ever-growing quantities of forms to be filled in.

A very intelligent-looking officer assures me that we had 800 large thirty-ton tanks in Belgium. They fought to the last tank, and must have done much damage to the Germans as they were far superior to theirs. What an avalanche of tanks the Germans must have had to overwhelm us!

Another officer gives us news received from Caen, describing how bad is the morale of the Germans, who hate the idea of attacking England by sea. And a very silent major only opened his mouth to say how tired he was of doing a useless, empty unproductive job. He had been forced to do it during the war at an Arsenal which manufactured little, and even that often badly. Nothing has changed; we have no sound ideas, and orders received are often contradictory and impossible to carry out. No! the new Government has not a good press.

During the last three days the Germans have launched a great aero-naval offensive against Great Britain. Having no wireless set capable of getting London on the short waves, I am reduced to reading the newspaper reports, which are so contradictory regarding the number of planes brought down and the general results obtained on land that it is impossible to know what to believe.

The Germans announce the destruction of very important ports after a day or two's bombing. I cannot believe it. I saw Dunkirk which was bombed and shelled by planes and guns in a very different way from the German attack on the British ports, because with an absence of aircraft and anti-aircraft guns, Dunkirk was at their mercy day and night for a fortnight. At the end, as was to be expected, the buildings near the port were destroyed, but the port was perfectly usable and 335,000 men were embarked in six to eight days, and a part of the town was still habitable.

But the number of naval vessels and, above all, freighters destroyed is alarming, if one is to believe the Germans. Admitting their figures to be very exaggerated, the real figures must be high and the losses irreplaceable. Fortunately the British have had additions to their fleet from Norway, Holland, Belgium and some vessels from Sweden and France. Will they be sufficient?

The general opinion is that the season is too far advanced for Germany to begin to attempt landings before the bad weather sets in, about 15 September. I hope that is so, for Great Britain, deprived of our help, must have so much to do before she possesses enough guns, tanks, munitions of every kind, and above all, planes; for her losses must be serious.

This evening, according to the communiqués, there is a lull in the fighting; the Germans have sent over only reconnaissance machines. Are they pausing to take breath? Or, as Jean Prouvost asks in *Paris-Soir* (has he changed his coat once more?), is something astir in the Balkans, are the concentrations of

Vichy

Russian troops near Rumania and Poland giving Hitler the same anguish as Napoleon felt when he was compelled to strike camp at Boulogne, because Austria had assembled fresh armies ready to strike him in the back?

I cannot let this too beautiful dream haunt me. Yet it seems impossible that Russia should not understand that once Germany has defeated England, she will be next on the list; the same applies to Italy, specialized in treason. She is quite capable of stabbing Germany in the back after having been her ally. No one can foresee the future. Let us wait and see.

To-day, 15 August, we barely met twenty cars on the road. It is by these signs that we realize how low we have fallen and how we are under the jack-boot of the Germans, who reserve the petrol for their armies.

16 *August* 1940.   Vichy. Pierre Masson is going to knock at the doors of the Ministry of Labour to try and get orders for his three hundred workmen. Nothing doing! The Colonel who receives him says: 'I have no work to distribute and no instructions; I myself want to know what I am to do.'

Cars in abundance in Vichy, all along the streets and in the public squares. The shortage of petrol is not felt here. The ladies' hairdressers are besieged by their clients, who wait hours for their turn. It would seem that the whole Garde Mobile of France is here; every fifty yards there are guards on duty, others stand by in reserve. Large numbers of others walk about in undress uniform waiting for their turn for duty. Why this fear? There are fewer dagoes about than before the war. Most of the thermal springs are closed and there are few people in the gardens. Everybody seems to be rushing about, the streets are thronged with men discussing important business or hurrying away to keep appointments with their attaché cases under their arms. Only the soldiers, including officers of all ranks, seem to lack something to do.

In the evening we arrive at Aurec on the banks of the Loire, passing through lovely country. No hotel or inn to be seen. If it were Switzerland or Alsace, or even the Jura, how different it would be! But here, nothing has been done to develop the hotel or touring industry.

18 *August* 1940.   One of Masson's engineers remembers that Barrault, a friend of his lately demobilized, spends his Sundays at Montrond, a little spa, 15 miles from Saint-Etienne. Barrault's brother, an engineer commander, has just returned from London, where he worked for the Intelligence. We go to Montrond, where we find Barrault, a charming fellow, and very likeable, at the swimming pool. A crowd of young men and women plunge into the water, reappear, then come ashore to sun-bathe. Barrault was a lieutenant in the Chasseurs Alpins; he relates a number of very amusing anecdotes of the attacks launched by the Italians during the three or four days between the signing of the armistice with the Germans and the Italians. Not once did the Italians, who had been told that the French fled at the sight of the enemy, come within gun-shot. The first time a 75 was fired, they put up their hands or lay flat on the ground, and cleared off by crawling away on their bellies. One of his friends and three poilus captured fifty Italians whom they had met, face to face, by giving them a few rounds with a revolver and ten from their rifles. The Italian captain said: 'Wait a minute, there are three more who are behind.' On the arrival of the laggards, our four men led the little band to our lines. On the whole, things are just the same as ever. The Italian air force is fairly accurate, but lacks dash and daring; their pilots run away before any old crate of ours.

Barrault phoned his brother, making an appointment for me with him to-morrow, Monday, in Lyons at 11 o'clock.

On returning from the swimming pool, Masson's engineer, Redlay, tells me that he was attached to the Arsenal at Roanne. All the plant was woefully old and worn out. Out of a battery of forty lathes, four or five remained in service. The worst were stripped down to provide spare parts for the remainder. On paper, 8000 shells a day were produced, but even on a good day only 1500 were actually turned out. Of the shells made, as many as 60 per cent were sometimes rejected and had to be melted down again. The old general commanding the Arsenal has been relieved of his duties and production had gone up. Redlay thinks that other arsenals had a better output.

19 *August* 1940. Arrived at Lyons. At 11 o'clock I meet Commander Barrault, handsome, young, full of vigour and enthusiasm. I question him on what he had seen in London. Immediately he goes full tilt at the British—whom he likes individually, but detests as a nation—and at de Gaulle. The British understood nothing about the war; they pushed us into it; they are our hereditary foe and are as much to be feared as the Germans. They are all under the thumb of the Freemasons and Jews. They have hardly any munitions, the Americans are delivering little in the way of planes, and manufactures from Canada are nil. Men aged twenty-seven are not even called up yet. If the British were the victors, their world-wide tyranny would break out again stronger than ever. (I do not know if the British tyrannized over us before the war, but we weren't unhappy in France under these shadowy tyrants.) The sole policy for our Government is not to help them to win, but to pray for the mutual exhaustion of the British and Germans, to such a point that we shall be able to resume the struggle (with what, he doesn't say) and so free ourselves from both tyrannies. In Sibylline phrases, he explains his return to France because he believes it possible to start fighting again and he gives one to understand that it would be with Russian aid. The British are a lot of children who imagine that they can fight parachutists with sporting guns.

He does recognize, however, that our Government travesties the truth when it states that the British did not give the help promised; on the contrary, they supplied two divisions more than agreed.

The de Gaulle movement is a joke; he is surrounded by dirty Jews; Admiral Muselier is a shady character and was fired. He was driven out of the Navy at the request of the British for misappropriation (and now they have accepted him as de Gaulle's right-hand man). De Gaulle's army is ridiculous, a mere flag, so that the British can say that the French continue to fight at their side. De Gaulle is a theorist, swollen with pride, who has not proved his mettle. (What about Abbeville, and Weygand's mention in dispatches?)

Barrault's special tale of woe is the ignoble action at Mers-el-Kébir, where, according to him, 1300 sailors died, drowned or burnt to death. Not a single senior officer of the Navy has agreed to remain with de Gaulle, only a few poor little midshipmen who have remained in London because of the girls. Those who have enrolled under de Gaulle regret it bitterly, or else they are ignorant simpletons. De Gaulle's associates are Jews, interpreters and chefs.

And yet Barrault is persuaded of the defeat of the Germans or at least of the check of their offensive against Britain, because they cannot get there before the equinoctial gales of 15 September, the latest date to ship over an invading army.

I try to persuade him that the British have a fine, well-equipped army, which fought well in Belgium; that in spite of all, our common enemy is Germany, who seeks our destruction and Great Britain's; that our interests are identical, and that despite old and new errors on the part of Britain, undeniably they are joint-authors with us of all the surrenders since the last war, they are partly responsible for events at Geneva, for our misunderstanding with Italy—all this I know as well as he does and any other Frenchman—yet our duty is to present a solid front to smash the power of the invader. Each time that I put forward one of these arguments, he gives me a look of hatred, draws back his lips and shows his teeth. I feel he would like to bite me, and see that it is useless to continue the discussion. I gave up trying to convert him and we parted after an hour and a half.

What is beneath it all? I wonder if Barrault had some unpleasant dealings with de Gaulle or with the British Government? The tone of his voice, the ridiculous pettiness of some of his quite childish arguments puts me on my guard. I can only explain his attitude by some unfortunate episodes which must have occurred while he was in London.

I leave for Marseilles in the evening, but I write to Barrault that he has converted me and that I am going back to Paris. He appeared to me such a suspicious character that I prefer to put him off the track. Lyons seemed well-nigh dead; very few cars, although the trams worked normally; few people in the streets and on the café-terraces. Business life and the factories seemed sluggish.

At the Hotel Bristol, near Perrache Station, a German mission is lodged whose duty is to supervise the Bron Flying field. Grey open German cars stand before the Hotel, transporting German officers and civilians beneath the very eye of the apparently uninterested population. Can it be true that the Germans have established a base of their own at Bron and at Clermont-Ferrand consisting of 200 machines sheltered from British bombing? Very unlikely, especially at Clermont-Ferrand, where I heard no mention of it, nor did I see a single German during the whole day.

20 *August* 1940.   Arrived at Marseilles at six o'clock. Rooms scarce. I manage to find one at 22 francs in the Hotel Beau-soleil, Gambetta Avenue; it is so narrow that I am obliged to put my suit-cases under the bed if I wish to reach the window.

The Quarter-Master's Department give me my ticket on the *Sidi-Brahim*, an auxiliary cargo boat of the Compagnie Générale de Transports Maritimes, sailing the day after to-morrow. Marseilles is lively; many people in the streets, trams and numerous buses, but very few cars. I am struck by the number of cinemas, all with low-priced seats, and the shops selling goods at one price.

A new feature of Marseilles is that the 'light' ladies have disappeared from the streets of the town. The ladies operate very discreetly now—in cafés.

22 *August* 1940.   Embarked at 11 o'clock with the 'mistral' blowing. There are twenty of us, first-class passengers, and four or five hundred Moroccans on the boat. Immediately they arrive, they place a rug on the deck and begin to play at tarot (card game). Money passes from hand to hand, and some will not have a sou left when they land. After about ten minutes a few passengers leave the dining saloon. We follow the coasts of France, then of Spain; this route, I am told, being imposed by the Admiralty and the Italians. We roll about during a part of the night to such an extent that the chairs on which the deck

passengers are lying perform some acrobatic feats. My suit-cases and shoes too. At three o'clock in the morning we pass Barcelona with its ramblas still alight.

We number six at our table, all demobilized officers; half pro-British, half anti-British. Discussions run high, but are very courteous. I meet Lagrave, a lieutenant who got his discharge in order to go to Tlemcen. In the morning, calm sea and splendid weather until five o'clock in the afternoon when we begin to roll in the Bay of Valencia.

24 *August* 1940.   Arrival at Oran at 12.30. From afar we see through glasses the *Dunkerque* which foundered at Mers-el-Kébir, and in the port of Oran war vessels which apparently suffered no damage. Some ten cargo boats have steam up, otherwise the port seems rather dead. Lagrave and I take two airy and spacious rooms, not dear, at the Continental with a view of the sea. Oran is not very lively, although the shops have fine displays. The Arabs are in the minority; a few veiled women. Here also are one-priced shops and the cinema reigns supreme.

25 *August* 1940. (*Sunday*.)   The street and the terraces are black with people, as soon as the sun goes down. Elegant girls and women, very well groomed, wavy hair, no stockings and toe-nails invariably red.

26 *August* 1940.   No chance of finding a boat for Gibraltar. We've drawn a blank. Lagrave and I decide to go on to Casablanca. The twenty hours' railway journey will be tiring, from half-past two this afternoon to ten o'clock to-morrow morning.

27 *August* 1940.   A pleasant journey; the train is fresh and airy and we number only four in the compartment. The hinter-land of Oran is very ugly, bare and burnt. Only the gorges near Tlemcen and the lovely olive groves nearby are pleasing to the eye. Night comes quickly. By the morning we have already passed Fez, and an immense dreary plain stretches away into the distance. We coast along a little wadi full of oleanders on which huge flocks of white ibises settle at times, like driven snow.

These ibises are very tame and will accompany flocks of sheep, goats and cows which seem to find their nourishment in the ground, for not a blade of grass is to be seen. The scattered tents of the Arabs are pitiable to see, so dirty and poor are they in appearance.

From the railway Rabat and Salé are dazzlingly white. But the almost total lack of trees spoils the picture for me. How beautifully the reds, mauves, yellows and ochres tone on the hills!

Casablanca is a splendid European town, quite new and admirably planned with gardens, arcades, wide and clean streets, but with no originality. The shops are very beautiful and the streets busy without having much traffic. Few Arabs except in the miserable little old Medina. Medina is characterless except for a fountain where about fifty Arabs, some of them handsome and covered in dreadful, gaudy rags, black-skinned, bare-footed, come to fill their enormous skin bottles made from whole goat-skins.

Lagrave and I began to look around, but without success. Our rooms at the Hotel du Touring, rue de l'Horloge, are large and comfortable for 25 francs. Quite handy is the Languedoc, little restaurant where we have quite good meals for 13 francs.

3 *September* 1940.   We make inquiries everywhere. At last I get my passport and hope to continue my task at Tangier or Larache. But I still need the police and above all the Spanish visas. Mr X., the Director of Y service, who has taken a liking to me, sends me to Mr Z., one of the Inspectors for the District. Unfortunately he says it would be useless for him to apply to the Spanish Consul to shorten my stay, as the French authorities stipulate a residence of fifteen days before giving a visa to a Spaniard, so the Spanish officials make the French wait a similar time by way of reprisals. Very intelligent, these petty vexatious measures! And we, who engage in this stupid little warfare, need the help of Spain above all.

Mr X. tells me that it is officially known that New Caledonia, our possessions in the Pacific, the Chad, Gaboon, all French Equatorial Africa, Congo, etc. have gone over to de Gaulle.

Others state that even Madagascar and Reunion have, too, but there is no confirmation of this. He listened in yesterday to London. Since Senegal, Morocco, Algeria, and Tunisia are contiguous, the movement should spread nearer and nearer.

Here there are many who do not seek to hide their feeling of confidence in Great Britain and de Gaulle—especially the older ones who went through the last war, the very young, and, of course, the Jews and Freemasons.

The Mers-el-Kébir affair, of which a garbled report has been circulated by Germany and the French Government, has done much harm to the cause of Great Britain. Were it otherwise, I think Morocco would have already come in. In that case, the whole of North Africa would rally, the war would assume another aspect and the Germans would be forced to occupy all France in order to guard and fortify the Mediterranean coastline, not forgetting Italy's 1250 miles. Perhaps ten divisions would be necessary; ten less at any rate to attack Great Britain.

Twenty divisions could be rapidly raised from the Chad and Senegal, Tripolitania could be taken from the hinterland, and the Italians cleared out of Africa. At once Victory would change sides; but we have signed our death-warrant by signing that shameful armistice.

Let the British continue to hold in Great Britain, let them continue to bomb Germany heavily. Already the defeatists are proving to be more cautious. They were prophesying Great Britain's downfall in less than no time, before the autumn, now they keep their mouths shut or talk of a war of attrition. Great Britain's resistance will stir up the fighting spirit of those who were down; they are only waiting for her first success and they will rush to take up arms again.

Here are a few examples which show the Government's general paralysis. Many women and children, and youths especially, have taken refuge in Morocco, thanks to steam-trawlers which set out from all the Breton ports and from Lorient in particular. Vichy will not allow these people to be repatriated without giving its sanction, but Vichy has not replied to a single request for six weeks, not a single permit has been given. Many of these unhappy people have no longer any money, the women who wanted to keep their boys aged 17 to 20 out of the clutches of the Boche have no news of their husbands and are greatly distressed. They are herded together in dormitories and their anger against the Government is genuine. All the youths, without exception, want to go to England. Three weeks ago, some of them got away, disguised as Foreign Legionaries, who are allowed to sail for England. But since then, this line of escape has been stopped, and the remainder are desperate at not being able to follow suit.

As I have no wireless, I am forced to get the news a day late from other people. It would seem that America, who can clearly be heard at nine o'clock, is drawing nearer to the British point of view. What a long time this nation takes to understand! Once again, let Great Britain stand firm, and America will regain confidence. They, too, believed in the invincibility of the Boche. A demonstration to the contrary is needed, and that London will give it is my firm hope.

Yesterday I went to Fedalla, some twenty miles to the north of Casablanca; its magnificent beach is as beautiful as La Baule's, as extensive and with sand as fine. While the country between Fedalla and Casablanca is grim and bare, Fedalla is a green oasis, elegantly laid out: lawns, gardens, palm-trees, eucalyptus and pines. Trees and flowers grow luxuriantly in the superb gardens of private villas, built by many people from Casablanca. On the esplanade stands the luxurious and delightful Hotel Miramar, in good colonial style; on its terrace one can while away delightful hours. The tiny old native town, a considerable distance from the new beach, has a certain air about it, with its embattled ramparts. But it is lousy! It takes courage to set foot in those parts, and you promise yourself a good scouring when you return, to rid yourself of all you've brought back. But the temptation is great!

A remarkable bouillabaisse is served up in the little restaurant where I take my meals, that is, lunch, for in the evening I eat only fruit, figs and grapes mostly, in my room.

A young pilot-officer told me this evening that a goodly number of planes have been flown over from Meknes and Marrakech to England. So now the amount of petrol for practice flights is limited, to stop the boys going a-gadding. All the same it is more honourable to have a dog-fight with a Messerschmitt than to run after the girls of Casa and Rabat. I wonder that those who remain haven't a permanent blush.

In the port I saw the *Jean Bart*, that enormous cruiser of 35,000 to 40,000 tons which, although it had not carried out its trials, preferred not to risk falling into Boche hands. So from Rochefort it sought the shelter of Casablanca. It has only two huge guns which, I believe, are without breech-blocks. A little farther away I counted eleven submarines, five or six destroyers, a small cruiser, the *Primauguet*, and a few other war vessels; together with a crowd of cargo-boats of all sizes, lying idle.

I have also seen the famous liner *Massilia*, where those members of the Government who refused to accept the Armistice and wished to continue the struggle from Morocco, had embarked. Violent scenes took place, I was told, when these Deputies had to land. Pétain has had them arrested or placed under police supervision in order to be able to bring them back to France before a Court of Justice. Their crimes? They probably want to continue fighting for their country....

Incidentally, many people look amazed when you tell them that the Republic exists no longer. The *coup d'état* was perpetrated so stealthily that the public was unaware that it had been done. The bloodless revolution seemed perfectly legal, because Parliament was summoned to ratify the list of appointments. Lebrun went, no drums or bugles rang out. Deputies and Senators, Herriot, Jeanneney continue to draw their salaries.

Old Moroccans say that the natives love France; they have no desire to see the Germans installed in their land. But the masses of the people care little. They hate the Roumis (Christians) and it matters little to them who is master; they don't want any of them. Yet the strength and the discipline of the Germans impress them. If only the poor devils knew what fate Hitler, with his racial ideas, had in store for them!

The fact is that Lyautey, that genial creative mind, did good work in his day. Not much has been done to improve the lot of the up-country Arab. His tent, his hut, his shack are pitiable. Why not make the proprietors, who amass enormous fortunes, build inexpensive, but decent three-roomed houses, in which they could lodge their workers? It wouldn't ruin them! In one year, a quarter of the population could be housed and the owner could supervise the cleanliness of the houses. They should be erected near to wells, and have cement floors. The master also should provide his workmen with one garment a year and those pitiful rags would be seen no more. In the towns, strips of material should be given to poor Arabs to enable them to patch their clothes. A fine should be imposed on the ragged, who, it must be admitted, appear to take pleasure in their unbelievable tatters. The poverty and misery of these poor creatures is a terrible thing, though some idiots call it local colour.

4 *September* 1940. I can now recognize the cries of all the street-vendors passing under my windows: the knife-grinder's reed-pipe, the old clothes man's 'Old clo's, old boots, old papers'.

I admire the perseverance of the old Jew second-hand clothes dealer who passes by five or six times a day almost at the double. How many miles does he do in the day, and how much does he earn?

Casablanca is certainly a very beautiful town. It is a pity that the roads weren't made wider still and more sites left for trees, grass, and flowers. Lyautey Park is most beautiful. But in the Centre and in the Boulevard de la Gare and the neighbouring avenues, a little greenness would have livened up the five, six, seven, even ten and eleven storeys of reinforced concrete which tire the eye and are lacking in any kind of visual freshness.

A great event! It has rained; the first rain since April falls on Casablanca—a great storm, plus a tornado whirling sheets of corrugated iron, planks and flower-pots through the air.

5 *September* 1940. Like autumn weather in France. A little rain, sky grey and low, and rather fresh.

America is on the war-path. She has just sent fifty destroyers to Great Britain. Great Britain holds firm and gives some hard knocks to Germany, who must now be beginning to have doubts about her famed lightning war against perfidious Albion. Berlin's daily broadcast that she has brought down hundreds of planes makes no difference to the British, who intensify each week their raids on numbers of towns in the Reich, Norway, Holland and France.

The long-range guns which shelled Dover didn't keep up the fire very long; one never hears them mentioned now. Hitler has spoken in Berlin. No longer is it a question of the 'blitz-krieg'; on the contrary, he says that the duration of the war is of little consequence, it is the result which matters. That's a new tune he's playing. The German soldiers in France were already complaining of time dragging in the month of July.

One of the latest British communiqués amused us by speaking of a possible German landing and said 'the warmest reception' ever known in history would be reserved for them.

Mr X. believes that when the armistice was signed Peyrouton, in conference with Le Beau, Governor of Algeria, Nogues of Morocco, uttered his famous words from Tunis saying that if France fell, the Empire stood and would continue to stand. After consultation, London is supposed to have declared that she couldn't help North Africa for six or eight weeks. With death in her soul, North Africa had to yield. How sad! But why should these people not throw off the Vichy and German yoke on the day when London can supply arms, munitions, aircraft and naval forces?

Mr X. also tells me that a few weeks ago, when contingents of Polish troops were embarking here on their way to England, a large number of young men, dressed in Polish uniforms, paraded the town, and slipped on board with the Poles. Others made for Agadir and thence with donkeys, three per man, one to ride and one each to carry food and water, they reached Senegal, travelling across the awful desert of Mauretania and following the coast—five weeks of suffering! What determination! What love for France!

What one may call propaganda of the purse is now on foot. The colonists are embittered by the impossibility of selling their produce; some of them have hundreds of thousands of francs' worth of wine or grain in their cellars and barns. Vegetables are being thrown away, owing to the shortage of shipping caused by the blockade.

New Medina

The word is passed from mouth to mouth that if Morocco rallied to the cause of de Gaulle, trade would be better than ever; this argument goes home. Besides, the *Moroccan Press*, the regular local paper which is of course pro-British, has published a leading article in which, although the case is not openly stated, one can nevertheless read between the lines. Moreover, the French paper *Gringoire*, which fills me with disgust by its grovelling to the Germans after long having poured out a stream of abuse, recognizes that the British are making a desperate effort at propaganda in Morocco. Or are the propagandists, patriotic Moroccans, working unaided?

I paid a visit to Casablanca's new Medina, the new Arab town. I have never seen anything more charming. The streets are clean, beautiful, and quiet, with fine Arab dwellings. Everywhere public fountains; no bad smells, but odours of musk and mint. The people are clean, and the ragged are in a minority. There are no Jews recognizable by their little black caps, as in old Medina, down by the port, which is lousy, dilapidated and smelly. The artisans work in their small shops, which are grouped by trades: here the smiths, there the joiners, over there the tailors sitting cross-legged in front of their Singer machines. In the pleasant covered markets are the sellers of djellabas and of brightly-coloured tunics, some of them in admirable taste and richly embroidered. Farther on are the carpet and tapestry merchants.

In the principal squares, the usual crowd of jugglers and snake-charmers entertain crowds of children, men and veiled women squatting round to listen to the never-ending stream of patter and jokes. When the collection comes, those who give their small change are always in the minority, but what does it matter? All performances are free.

I spent some delightful hours there. In new Medina, numbers of Arab women may be seen, in the European town too, well dressed and of distinguished appearance with their pretty dove-grey djellabas, tailored to perfection, and their veils of fine hand-made lace, well adjusted under the eyes, their little feet, with slender, henna-dyed heels, in embroidered native slippers. Their laughing eyes, almost innocent of make-up, command admiration.

Weygand for North Africa

At the central market, a few yards from my hotel, the prices would send French housewives into a beautiful dream—even though they have doubled within the last few years. An exquisite leg of mutton cost 15 francs a kilo and that is the dearest joint you can buy; eggs, 5 francs a dozen. Very fine soles, 17 francs a kilo; ordinary fish: dorado, splendid red mullet from 3 to 5 francs a kilo; tomatoes 1 franc, figs 2 francs, and so on. And they complain here of the high cost of living. It is the same everywhere. In a family food works out at ten francs per head. What would our Parisians think of that?

6 *September* 1940.   My activities leave me a considerable degree of leisure. I go and sit in the Lyautey Park, near the garden reserved for children. All sorts of games are provided: toboggans, wooden-horses, swings, running tracks, etc. This is a fresh spot with lovely green, shady lawns. The entrance fee is nominal. I see beautiful little fair heads, which remind me of my son, who is now 25, in the forces, and from whom I have had no news. He was in the Maginot Line and must have been taken prisoner. And when shall I know the fate of my nieces, their mother, my dear Ghislaine, and their father, who was a lieutenant in a colonial regiment?

This evening I listened in to London on a neighbour's wireless. Indo-China was referred to as if it had rallied to the government of 'all the Free French under General de Gaulle'; if this is really true, it would be a first-class trump card.

7 *September* 1940.   The newspapers announce that General Weygand has been appointed delegate of the Government in North Africa. It must be because de Gaulle's movement is extending and worrying Vichy. In spite of all the respect I have for Weygand, I cannot forget that he presided over the War Council for long years and did nothing to change our policy of *laissez-aller*. He is moreover an old man of 74 or 75, very young for his age, so they say, but he lives on his past, on his name. Has he shown in this war, as generalissimo, a single stroke of genius? We, on our side, stood our ground in Belgium and on the Somme,

and de Gaulle smashed the German front with his division, and advanced 9 miles. But others on his left and right did not follow up the good work. I know that the fight was all but lost, and that his army was withdrawing, but was he the man to stop the rot? God knows, I was filled with hope when I heard of his appointment. No longer can I believe in him, nor in the virtue of words and names; only the courage born of tanks and aeroplanes will suffice. Weygand brings us only a worn-out name, outworn twenty years ago.

The Government has been reshuffled; already! There were too many square pegs in round holes. It was plain to everyone. The newspapers publish nothing but lists of the Government's nominees. Scant news!

The Government has certainly done some good work; the abolition of the privilege allowed to home-distillers, greater freedom to religious organizations in teaching and a few other measures. But there is nothing original in these ideas; they only express what thirty million French people have been demanding for thirty years. But of new ideas, new measures, new organization, there is no trace. All that has been done is to abolish the most flagrant abuses. It is always easier to pull down than to put up. But the sad thing is that, as the Government is unpopular, even the best reforms will be unpopular too. The Government is favourable to a new religious spirit; it will end by creating a fresh wave of anti-religious feeling.

It is true that refugees have been brought back to their homes, and soldiers too, but there is nothing wonderful in that. Demobilization was, in fact, a mass of indecision and muddle. The unfortunate officers who had to carry it out could not understand anything, each order being immediately followed by a counter-order. The Government instructions were so confused that, as I have already said, the men demobilized themselves, and the refugees frequently did the same.

London is standing up to terrible bombing, she is even returning bomb for bomb on Berlin, Hamburg and on all the big cities of Germany. She sets fire to forests. Let her continue and gradually other colonies will rally to her. Her communiqués are always humorous and gay. Is it genuine, or just swagger?

Rabat and Salé

8 *September* 1940.   Spent Sunday at Rabat and at Salé. The loveliest nooks in tiny Rabat are the Oudaias, the remains of the ramparts of the old palace of the Sultan. Flowers everywhere and a fine view over the Oued and Salé. I visited the old palace; marvellous rugs, arms, and jewels, all in good taste. What splendid art! From the top of the ramparts, the little Arab guide showed me the whole town standing in dazzling whiteness on the hill-side.

'The great Mosque of the Roumis.'

'The Cathedral?'

'Yes, sidi, and there is "Sultan Nogues" Palace.'

The quarter of the town containing the official residences is admirable. Each block of ministerial offices is of a different shape, but always in the Arab style, with lovely inner courts, and fountains playing in the middle of large gardens artistically designed and in splendid order. Enough water is poured on them each day to make the fortune of four or five hundred market gardeners and their families. But that is another matter. Hundreds of millions have been spent in constructing what is a veritable city; but one has to admit, something perfect has been created.

Rabat lies rather huddled within its massive walls and lacks beauty, especially when one remembers Avignon, Carcassonne and particularly Aigues-Mortes.

I much preferred Salé on the other side of the Oued, which you can cross for twopence in a small boat. Salé is strongly native within its gay walls, teeming with people, and relatively clean. I never tire of watching the tradesmen, especially the tailor, surrounded by his helpers, little boys sewing sedately, while others hold the quadruple strands two or three yards away from the tailor and cross them over after every stitch made by the master, as automatically as a machine. The tailor is often the schoolmaster; ten or twelve youngsters sit gravely round him, chanting the alphabet which they follow on large cards resting on their knees. They look charming with their pretty intelligent faces, their heads shaven except for a plaited mesh on the top and a little to the right.

I chatted on the outward and homeward journeys in the coach

with Mlle Y., a very intelligent French girl, radiologist to a
doctor in Casablanca for the last ten years. She assures me that
the pro-de Gaulle feeling is spreading rapidly and that the Army
officers generally are fuming because they hadn't a chance to
fight. They would be particularly pleased if they could have a
smack at the Italians, whom they despise. She corroborates the
fact that many airmen have flown, and still fly, their machines
over to Gibraltar. Washington has announced by radio that
twenty-nine machines have just left Morocco. Goebbels has
threatened to occupy North Africa if the pro-British demon-
strations continue. All this would seem to agree with the
appointment of Weygand as the Government's delegate in
Africa, and the disaffection of the Chad and of French Equatorial Africa.

Mlle Y. complains of the doubtful taste of the British slogans
broadcast at eight o'clock each evening. We are suffering and do
not feel in the mood to joke. We want information and cheering
up, that is all.

At Rabat, I did not see any shops closed for having illegally
raised prices. This happened at Casablanca, where half the shoe
shops, a few men's outfitters and a small number of food shops
were closed down for a week or a fortnight, with an obligation to
pay the whole staff during that time. Prices are strictly controlled at Casa, and so living is not dear. So few women wear
stockings that not a single shop specializing in stockings exists.
They are never displayed in shop windows.

10 *September* 1940.   I have all my visas and leave for Tangier
to-night at 8.30.

11 *September* 1940.   I did not know that a permit was necessary to take away money. The French Customs at Soul-el-Arba
confiscated from me 4700 francs and £3. But I am informed that
I shall quickly recover the money on making application.

The plain over which we have been travelling since dawn in
Spanish Morocco is as ugly, as arid as any in the French zone.
Sheep and sorghum are almost the only source of wealth.

After the inevitable dispute with the taxi-driver, who de-

mands 30 francs and to whom I give ten—twice as much as is
usual—I take a room at the Hotel Valentin but shall not stay.
Too dear, too old and too overrun with ants, which have to be
sprayed twice a day. They are everywhere, in my luggage; the
fruit that I put on the chest of drawers is black with them in five
minutes. The clients consist of Englishmen, old and young, but
there are not many of them.

I hasten to see the British Consul. He is very kind and wel-
comes me, but pours cold water on my plans, for he has no
instructions and no means of helping me. The only way of
reaching England is, at one's own expense, to go by air to Lisbon,
then on by boat to England. Cost: 9000 to 10,000 francs. I am
500 francs short of that, even if I get back my 4700 francs. What
can I do? Gibraltar is inaccessible. 'There are hundreds like
you,' says the Consul, 'London tells me to keep you waiting; no
date has been fixed, nor is there any certainty of transport.' I
am completely bowled over. I go to the Moroccan State Bank
and make application for the return of my meagre funds which
were confiscated. I am told that I shall have them in three or
four days.

12 *September* 1940.　I have again visited the British Consul,
who has undertaken to forward to General de Gaulle a letter and
certain secret plans of special apparatus of which I am the
bearer. I beg the General to help me to get to England; I tell
him I am ready to serve even as a private soldier.

I wander about Tangier completely at a loss. It is a charming
little town perched on the hill-side. You spend your whole
time going up and down hill. Except for a part of the town,
where beautiful villas remind you of almost any town on the
Cote d'Azur, the European and Arab dwellings are mingled
everywhere; so too are parasol pines, acacias, palm trees and
eucalyptus trees. The Arabs here are very europeanized. Many
women wear shoes instead of babouches. Much French is spoken
and the names of the main streets are written, first in French,
then underneath in Spanish and Arabic. The town swarms with
clean people, and I didn't meet any ragged folk. Everywhere
Moroccan soldiers, with slung rifles, in espadrilles (rope soled

canvas shoes) and puttees, police the streets. They have a fine bearing. There are also squads of 'babillas', as they would be called in Italy, youngsters aged eight to twelve, wearing red berets, marching along, singing a war song and carrying rifles taller than themselves.

The bay is very lovely; from the fine, hard sandy beach stretching in an immense arc and very shut in, and particularly from the little port now deserted, the view in the evening is splendid. To the left, in the blue distance, stands Spain; to the right, in the background, are the blurred outlines of the Rif mountains. In the front rises the exceedingly white town, with vestiges of old walls, clumps of trees, large hotels and native houses dotted everywhere. Lastly thousands of white stones—the Moslem cemeteries—cover many an acre.

At night, life seems to be still more intense. The money-changers, the shops ablaze with light displaying their silks, babouches, groceries, the hairdressers and cafés remain open until a very late hour and seem full of customers.

13 *September* 1940.   The British Consul has taken my letter and the photographs of the apparatus of which I have the plans for General de Gaulle. I shall wait here hoping to hear soon from de Gaulle.

The Consul knows that the British communiqués do not say everything. But what they say is exact. So much the better. For Winston Churchill has made a very fine speech once more to warn the British that an early attempt at invasion on the part of the Germans is quite a possibility; it may come to England, Ireland and Scotland at the same time. All the ports from Norway to the Bay of Biscay are black with German barges and boats, and everywhere troops are massed ready. Great Britain awaits them with stout hearts; should they succeed in landing, every village and house will be defended. Churchill has declared also that for every plane lost, three German planes will be brought down, for every pilot lost, five German pilots will perish. If that is true, as the Consul believes, what slaughter for the Germans !

The army of occupation

The R.A.F. bombing raids over Germany show no signs of slackening. A good omen!

In France the Government has once more changed its representative at the Armistice Commission. To solve the unemployment problem, they have a brain-wave; they are going to undertake work on a very large scale.

The army of occupation is costing us 20 million marks a day, or 400 million francs, or 144 milliards a year. What numbers of aeroplanes, tanks, and guns could have been manufactured with that formidable sum! Heavens, where are we going?... What a fine piece of work is this armistice which is destined to set France on her feet so that the Germans may bleed her to the last drop of blood. I have an interesting booklet given to me by the Consul, on the Brest-Litovsk treaties of 1917 and 1939. With what cynical brutality have the Germans robbed Rumania, Russia and the Balkans! All that was blotted out by the Treaty of Versailles. But to those who complain of their fate, the Germans reply: 'What are you complaining about? We have given you generous and humane conditions. You see how we shall treat France and Great Britain.'

Germany hasn't changed; we shall see, in fact.

But the author foresees that the last word has not been spoken by Russia, and that Hitler cannot feel entirely reassured. Nor Stalin, for he must have a suspicion that Germany will try to stake a claim on the territories acquired from the Baltic countries, Poland and Rumania. I have always thought that not all the cards have been played, either by Russia, or by America.

I've bought a bathing costume and spent the morning in the water and on the sand. A very windy day.

14 *September* 1940. I've moved to the Family Hotel, Boulevard d'Espagne, a former villa transformed into a family boarding-house. I have two huge rooms on the second floor with every comfort; a bit shabby, it is true, but with a large window overlooking the sea and bay. Rent 10 francs a day. I have paid for a fortnight in advance. I am much more comfortable than at the Valentin, and there are no ants.

Disappointed hopes

My great hope has been dashed to the ground. I thought I should be able to go from Lisbon to London by boat, the cost being £15 first-class, £10 second-class, and I discover that the maximum number of francs to the £ is 150. Unfortunately, neither Cook's, nor any shipping company will guarantee a passage, and the Portuguese Consul requires a guaranteed passage from America or another continent before granting his visa. I shall go into the matter on Monday.

After my bathe, I stayed a good hour watching the fishermen dragging their nets, with a good quantity of sardines, red and grey mullets. But this evening I suffer from severe sunburn on my arms and back.

German raids over England slowed down yesterday, but the Italians announce the beginning of their offensive against Egypt.

19 *September* 1940.   Lagrave joined me yesterday. He was delayed by the Spanish visa. The Portuguese Consul has agreed to send my request for a visa to Lisbon so that I can pay a visit to the representative, in that town, of the Company of whom I am the so-called general agent for Morocco. I have to wait ten to fifteen days for the reply. I have to be photographed, and I realize once again that passport photos aren't much use for making conquests.

London has held in check the German bombers. Yesterday 184 Boche machines were brought down; a fine day's hunt!

The French Government is more and more worried over the attitude of North Africa and particularly Morocco which it will defend, so it says, against all aggression, no matter whence it may come. A business man from Casablanca whom I met in the train to Tangier estimates that a month ago 25 per cent were pro-British and 75 per cent against. To-day these figures would be 60 and 40.

Perhaps the Germans will invade us here, pretending that they are merely forestalling the British—a tale we heard in Norway, Holland, Belgium. But here they have to reckon with Gibraltar and the Royal Navy.

The Italians have advanced along the coast in the desert

which separates Cyrenaica from Egypt, a distance of 440 miles.
The British have retired without fighting, having room to do so.
They will engage in battle only on the terrain chosen by them.
The newspapers spread the idea that the Germans, having had
to put off their invasion of England until next spring, which is a
great moral check for them, will probably use the winter months
by assisting the Italians in their Egyptian campaign. In my
opinion there are three reasons against this: (1) The Italians will
be afraid that once the Germans are installed in Egypt they
won't budge. (2) If the Germans are to do everything themselves, they have no cause to pay the Italians for a show of help.
It would serve only to prove the congenital incapacity of the
Italian soldier, who is admirable before a camera and passable
before negros armed with bows and arrows. (3) With the British
fleet in the Mediterranean, how will they be able to transport
heavy reinforcements?

20 *September* 1940.   By a surprising coincidence, I shall perhaps have all my long-standing difficulties solved in a few days.
I hardly dare rejoice, but all the same, I have a feeling of well-
being unknown to me, alas, for several months.

From my window I watch the night enveloping Spain which
is so near that you fancy you could almost touch it with your
hand. A Spanish cruiser at anchor in the port, a museum piece,
is lighting its riding-lights. Everything suggests tranquillity,
but I feel terribly excited.

22 *September* 1940.   The Government has dismissed the civic
councils directed by some of the bosses of the former Republic:
Herriot, Tasso, Hellen Prévost, Max Dormoy. It is hard luck
for them especially for big 'father' Herriot.

Food restrictions will be severe in France this winter if one
judges by the quantities allowed to each ration card for meat,
fats, etc. Fortunately my sister has a little store, as many
others have, I hope. Moreover, the garden of our little country
house should keep her supplied with vegetables.

Monsieur Arditti has given Lagrave and myself some very
reassuring news. He thinks that Egypt has nothing to fear; if

they had, troops would have been sent there. The British will attack the Italians when they are ready. He thinks that Great Britain has just reached parity with Germany in the manufacture of aeroplanes. In London they are preparing raids over Berlin which will last 24 hours out of 24. In the spring, British aviation will clearly be on top. But he thinks that the war will last several years, and that Germany will collapse suddenly, as in 1918.

Lagrave has met the Comte de Paris, with whom he talked for a good half hour. The Comte believes there will shortly be a movement in the colonies in favour of de Gaulle, of course. He hopes to ascend the throne of France after the victory of which he has no doubt.

Nor has Monsieur Arditti, who has drawn us a magnificent picture of British morale. Here is one example taken from a thousand: the Germans, hoping to crush the British fighting spirit, have just sunk on a stormy night a boat loaded with children en route for Canada. It was an act of savagery, there were 200 victims. A mother and five of her little ones perished; their house in London had been destroyed. The father, a worker in a factory and an old 1914 campaigner, immediately joined up to avenge his family.

Monsieur Arditti is also persuaded that all the figures and information given by the British are exact. Besides, the press, except for censored military news, is absolutely free to make what comments it likes, free even to attack the Government. But these attacks are all directed to the same end: to urge the Government to make greater efforts and to increase war production.

The Germans by their attacks on Buckingham Palace and on boats loaded with evacuated children commit a psychological error. They stiffen the resistance of all subjects of the Empire.

A great effort is being made here to combat German propaganda. A pro-British paper, having a circulation of 500 copies a month ago, now prints 3000, and people fight to get them.

Indo-China has given in to Japan, who will establish air bases, with a view to Singapore as much as to China, and will have a right of way for her troops. Japan feels the American Giant coming perilously near and would like to finish with Chiang-Kai-Shek. From Tongking, Japan will be able to bomb the Burma road, the only route by which Chiang-Kai-Shek can receive arms and munitions from America. For France it is a new humiliation and probably the beginning of the end of our domination in Indo-China. The Japanese, despite the assurances they have given, will not let go their prey. They used the same methods twenty years ago in Manchukuo.

23 *September* 1940.   The Comte de Paris was not mistaken. De Gaulle has sailed with a British Squadron and troop transports to Dakar which he has begun to shell. Galandou-Diouf called him, but the new Governor Buisson, following Vichy's instructions, has refused to hand over the town. I imagine that resistance will be for form's sake if the country, stirred up by Galandou-Diouf, is favourable to de Gaulle.

The consequence may be immensely important, for this operation, if isolated, would be meaningless. First the whole of French Equatorial Africa would rally to the good cause. Great Britain would next hope to have the support of North Africa; the whole of the continent would be in the hands of de Gaulle and the British. To throw out the Italians, who would be cut off from their Metropolis, seems possible; who can say? Perhaps it would mean a separate peace with Italy, as Commander Barrault suggested, next spring. It would be a complete change of the situation—as I predicted several days ago.

De Gaulle would gain in prestige, and Great Britain couldn't fail. He wouldn't have put himself at the head of the expedition if he couldn't bring it to a successful issue.

What will be Spain's attitude if de Gaulle enters Morocco? Franco fears the Reds, who must be chafing at the bit and only waiting for a chance of revenge. Some people state that there are between 100,000 and 300,000 soldiers in Spanish Morocco ready to invade if we move. Gibraltar and the British fleet would render a landing of any size, plus the continuous flow of supplies necessary in modern warfare, extremely hazardous. Would the risk be worth taking? What would be the gain?

Would he hope to get French Morocco? The Germans are after that.

Franco will possibly allow the German army to pass through Spain, but the Germans are faced with the same problem of landing here as they are in England. It would take months of organization. There are no ports, near enough at least, in the south of Spain capable of handling heavy traffic. If Great Britain could supply tanks, aeroplanes and arms to the troops that could be recruited in hundreds from Morocco, Algeria and Tunisia, the battle in this corner of the world would be won. De Gaulle would perhaps establish the government of the French Empire in Algiers.

The inhabitants of Tangier are very excited by the news of the attack on Dakar. There is the additional fact that motorized columns could invade the whole of Morocco via Senegal in a few days. Casablanca could be taken from the land, and there would be no landing difficulties. The British Navy would only have to block the port to prevent boats from escaping. And if the Germans had the idea of invading Morocco they would find themselves 1200 to 1800 miles from their base and from their factories. In France the railways would be sabotaged, I hope, and in the factories the workmen would ca' canny. The Germans would have to use up a part of their invasion force intended for Great Britain. How would they be able to bring barges and motor-boats in sufficient quantities to Spain? In any case Germany would be going still farther afield, and thinning out her forces over vast areas, from Norway to Morocco passing through Poland and the Balkans. A worse situation than Napoleon ever had to face, and he fell.

Germany certainly reckoned on Great Britain's collapse following that of France. But the British bull-dog does not let go the bone as quickly as Pierre Laval and Marquet.

By the way, what does Weygand, in a nursing home (where he is recovering from a car accident), think of operations in Africa, the government of which is in his keeping?

Raids on Great Britain have slowed down lately, losses in machines on both sides are now insignificant. The Germans must have suffered terrible losses in the past, for a few days ago they issued an order calling up the pilots of the last war. A bad sign for them!

If de Gaulle and Great Britain start a campaign in Africa, does that not show that they do not fear an immediate German invasion in Great Britain? Probably the weather, and the considerable amount of damage done to Boche barges and boats assembled in the invasion ports, has something to do with it. Lagrave, whom I meet regularly at lunch time, showed me a paper displaying a great headline: 'Ex General de Gaulle' and 'French Indo-China'. It must be a printer's mistake, he says, it should read: 'Ex French Indo-China' and 'General de Gaulle'.

25 September 1940.   Everything has suddenly come right for our journey. Lagrave and I will be at the end of our wanderings before the end of the month, thanks to Lagrave, who is arranging for the cost of our passages, by air, from Lisbon to Great Britain to be paid in England.

The most confusing news is going round concerning the attack on Dakar. It seems that at first sight de Gaulle thought that he would be welcomed with open arms, that resistance would be merely for form's sake and that the de-Gaullistes would force the Governor to capitulate. At the present moment, one cannot conceal the fact that the set-back has been at least a moral one; it is possible that the Government, now wide awake, may have taken appropriate steps to break the resistance of de Gaulle's followers.

I do not think that the game is up as far as the British are concerned; first because their prestige would suffer, next because of the extreme importance of Dakar. It is one of the few ports where boats coming from India to England, via Cape Town, can put in, coal or take in oil. Freetown is near, but I doubt whether it is as well equipped. Dakar is above all an advanced spur in the Atlantic, the nearest point to the American continent and for nothing in the world would they like to see it in enemy hands.

I have seen and heard squadrons of French aeroplanes setting out from Morocco on their way to bomb Gibraltar. To-day twenty-seven planes passed over between three and four o'clock. They came back individually, probably having been broken up by A.A. fire. What a sad sight! To think that those shells and bombs were intended for the Germans and are now being used by the French against the British. How distressing and stupid! Here people talk of nothing else, but as the police are very active, the conversation is very reserved.

27 *September* 1940. All is ready. We have our visas and take the aeroplane which leaves here for Lisbon at 3 o'clock. Mr Guinfolleau, manager of Cook's-Wagons-Lits-Air France, has helped us considerably, although he is French. But he is not a Vichy Frenchman, as the English say contemptuously.

I lighten my luggage considerably, keeping only one case. Only 15 kilogs (33 lb.) are allowed free, all extra luggage costing 10 escudos or 31 francs the kilog. The journey from here to Lisbon is rather dear, 3200 francs for a flight of two to three hours. Thanks to Lagrave's sharing funds, we shall be able to reach England. It will cost us more than 12,000 francs each just for the aeroplane fares alone from here to Great Britain. At last I shall be able, if I wish, to take dinner in the evening; I needn't wash my linen myself, or deprive myself of a newspaper or a cup of tea. I am not sorry that I have had to count every sou, otherwise I shouldn't have got this far.

This morning a magnificent view at sunrise. From my window I see the whole stretch of water tinted with the most delicate colours from a pale rose to the darkest indigo. To the left the Spanish coast sheers away revealing the Atlantic; to the right, the huge jagged line of the rock of Gibraltar stands out at the entrance to the Bay of Algeciras and the Mediterranean disappears over the horizon. You must see the Rock to realize the immense importance of its position; it is a safety bolt that the British can shoot at will.

De Gaulle's action at Dakar has definitely failed. It is very serious from the point of view of morale and probably also from the strategical side. The British account frankly admits that as there was resistance, the taking of Dakar would have necessitated a major military operation. De Gaulle and Churchill were deceived by the too optimistic reports and their preparations were not on a large enough scale. Galandou-Diouf sent a message of loyalty to Vichy forty-eight hours after the operation had begun. Did he send a similar message to de Gaulle three weeks before? Did he run with the hare and hunt with the hounds? And when he saw the action taking a turn for the worse, did he try to save his skin, and his future? I shall try to discover the truth when I arrive in England.

A nasty blow for de Gaulle's prestige. Vichy and the Germans will make the most of it. All my hopes are dashed to the ground, for the moment at least. If Great Britain ever opens up similar operations in the future, it will be harder, for Vichy will start improving the defences; and success will make the defenders more daring, and de Gaulle's followers more timid.

A British communiqué confirms the news that a few weeks ago the Royal Navy prevented French warships from descending on French Equatorial Africa, which has definitely gone over to de Gaulle. Will his set-back modify the attitude of French Equatorial Africa, Chad, etc....?

The R.A.F. continues to bomb Berlin and all Germany with the utmost vigour. Are the Italians consolidating the 45 miles of desert which they occupy on the road to Cairo or are they held up by the twin bombardments of fleet and air force? Just at present, they are lying low.

Departure from the poor little airfield at Tangier at five in the afternoon, one hour late, because just as we were about to take off, one of the plane's motors caught fire. On the flying ground I meet the British Consul, who tells me that he has just received a telegram from Admiral Muselier (in the absence of de Gaulle) ordering me to be sent to England immediately; the letter to de Gaulle and the special information that the Consul forwarded for me are certainly responsible for this. Its nice to be able to look forward to being sympathetically received on arriving.

After two and a half hours of flight over the Spanish coast-line, then over Portugal, we land at Cintra, twelve miles from Lisbon. We learn that all the hotels in Lisbon are full, so Lagrave and I find comfortable rooms at the Hotel Nuñes at Cintra.

28 *September* 1940.   All's well.   Imperial Airways inform us that all seats are booked up a month in advance. But the British

Lisbon

Embassy, to whom we turn, sends us to the Military and Air Attachés. On returning in the afternoon to Imperial Airways, we learn that they have received an order from the Embassy to reserve seats for us on the following Tuesday. So only three days to wait here.

So much the better from all points of view, for our resources would not allow us a longer stay. The rate of exchange is at rock-bottom; we receive 26 escudos for 100 francs. At lunch in a very modest restaurant some fried whiting costs me 16 francs, a slice of pork with a few potatoes 28 francs. Living as meanly as possible we spend 250 francs a day.

Lisbon and its port on the Tagus are very impressive. It is an old town, picturesque, very busy, and enriched by the war. It is the only great port of western Europe through which Great Britain can trade and breathe. Numbers of new American cars everywhere, and intense sea traffic.

A real joy to us is that it is cool and raining a little. No more of that inexorable blue sky; the damp air has a pleasant smell; there are trees, real trees, with branches, and not those loppy feather dusters called palm-trees, nor tired-looking eucalyptus trees.

On our return to Cintra, we have time to visit the ancient Royal Palace, a patchwork building, half Arab, half European, ten centuries old in certain parts. The interior has been converted into a museum containing a few extraordinary things.

To-morrow, Sunday, we will walk to Montserrate, 2 or 3 miles away, to see the park surrounding the castle. It is said to be a marvellous place and I should very much like to see it because of Farrère's fine description in his interesting novel, *Le Chef*.

If I am not tired—I have had dysentery for a fortnight owing to the magnesium in the water of Morocco, also to an excess of fruit and hotel food—I shall visit the Royal Palace of La Plena, whence the last king fled. I believe that it has a lovely park, as seen from a distance. Now that I have left Morocco I realize that it is a very attractive country on the screen and on picture postcards, but I shall never desire to return there, still less to live there.

The *Daily Mail*, three days old and costing 4·80 francs, says

that Daladier has no intention of being garrotted at Riom without defending himself; and for that, he will attack Pétain and
Weygand, who had made out reports to him stating the excellent condition of the Army, and our perfect preparation for war.
If anyone is guilty, even more than the civilians, it is the military
clan, the Army Council, now enthroned at Vichy. If anyone is to
be tried, let them be indicted, as well as many other members of
the present Government. The long and short of it is that both
French and British statesmen failed to understand Germany,
failed to understand what the next war would be like. Riom
serves only to lull public opinion, by offering it a scape-goat, and
probably a few personal scores will be paid off, as from one
political shark to another.

It is all a very ugly business. But until I have proof to the
contrary, I shall always believe that Daladier, Mandel and
Reynaud were honest men and worked as well as a rotten system
would let them.

29 *September* 1940.   Visited this morning the admirable park
of Montserrate, but not the castle, which is inhabited by an
Englishman, a Mr Cook. A wild ravine clothed with a luxuriant
tropical and European vegetation; chestnuts, cocoa-nut palms
and banana trees; tree-ferns side by side with oaks and all kinds
of pines. Water everywhere, flowers superlatively beautiful and
on the horizon the sea. Farrère was right.

Gibraltar has been bombed again by the French, the very day
after Pierre Laval had visited Paris. It makes one think that he
went there on German orders and was compelled to toe the line.
Where is such a policy leading France? This attack on Gibraltar,
three days after the departure of the British squadron from
Dakar, cannot be considered as a way of making the British let
go their grip. Nor can it be treated as an isolated fact, but
rather it is part of the German plan, which Pétain and his
Government abjectly execute, to set the English and French
against each other. Pétain under the German heel, and taking
orders from the Germans! What degradation!

But if France takes up arms against Britain it will probably
hasten the entry of America into the war; already since the

By air from Lisbon

signing of the military alliance between Japan and the Axis powers she has gone far along that road. The Committee for Common Defence of Canada and the United States has held a special session. It is my impression that things are going to happen.

Monsieur Arditti assured me, when I was in Tangier, that 500 pilots, Norwegians, Czechs, etc., have finished their training in Canada and are going to fly over the latest types of machines. Bravo !

30 *September* 1940. We have our passport visas—not without many difficulties. Our seats are reserved on the aeroplane which leaves to-morrow morning and will land us, if all goes well, in the evening, in England.

The French Government having revoked its treaty of Commerce with Portugal (why, I cannot understand), the visa which was formerly free now costs, at the current rate of exchange, 310 francs.

The Portuguese papers say that Great Britain has sent an ultimatum to Madagascar to compel her to form an alliance with her. It is not known what attitude the Colony will take. Perhaps the ultimatum is the reply to yesterday's bombing of Gibraltar. Great Britain, it is clear, seeks to assure herself of ports of call on the India, Cape of Good Hope route: Diego Suarez, Majunga, in Madagascar; Cape Town in South Africa and Dakar in Senegal. She is wise.

To-morrow evening, after eight to ten hours' flying, Lagrave and I will sleep in England. At last, but what a business to get there !

1 *October* 1940. Departure at 8.30 a.m. in a Dutch plane from the Lisbon Airport. Fill up with petrol near Oporto. We follow the beautiful mountainous coast of Portugal. Then we fly over the ocean at a height of 8000 feet; beneath us—unforgettable sight—are lovely cumulus clouds which seem to rest on the waves. Patches of blue peep through; it is the sea down below shining in the sunshine. I was reminded too of vast fantastic icebergs floating in polar seas.

England at last

Later our journey resembled a winter sports scene draped with a magnificent azure sky; the sea of clouds uniform, almost smooth, and so compact that if one were forced to land there, one would have no fear, as it would seem just like coming to rest on skis or luge.

As we approach England, we come down from 8000 feet to 1000 feet. The windows are blacked-out with plywood in order to hide the naval defences from the passengers. We arrive at five o'clock in the evening. The police closely question us and the customs search is thorough, but that merely gives us confidence. We are warmly welcomed; tea and cakes are served to all the passengers.

In the plane there are three of us, all come for the same purpose, Lagrave and I to enter the service once more, and a Belgian who is going to join his contingent.

Finally Lagrave and I are taken to the hotel, which is very large and comfortable. The dinner is abundant and well prepared.

Ten o'clock and the sirens are wailing. I am tired and have no wish to go down to the shelter.

To-morrow morning we go to General de Gaulle's Headquarters in London.

The police have taken from me the drawings of a flame-thrower that I brought from France and of which I made a report to General de Gaulle, while at Tangier. They will send my records so that the General will have them before I arrive. They are quite right to take such infinite precautions.

And now I am going to sleep my first night in England, since Dunkirk.

THE END

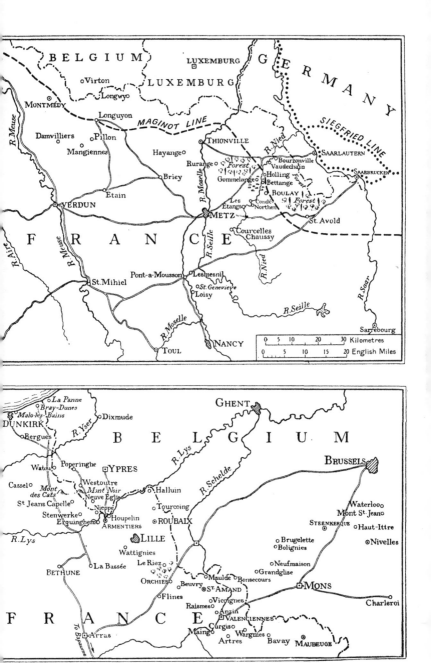

The Scenes of Battle